Science Arena

Dave Rear

最新科学の探求

S SEIBIDO

音声ファイルのダウンロード／ストリーミング

CD マーク表示がある箇所は、音声を弊社 HP より無料でダウンロード／ストリーミングすることができます。下記 URL の書籍詳細ページに音声ダウンロードアイコンがございますのでそちらから自習用音声としてご活用ください。

http://seibido.co.jp/ad601

Science Arena

To Teachers and Students

The world of science and technology never sits still. Whether it concerns computers, robots, transportation, space, sports, health, or the environment, human beings are always pushing the boundaries of what is possible, seeking new ways to improve our lives and extend our knowledge. This book looks at some of the most interesting and exciting developments that are taking place in science today.

It is divided into five main sections, each with four units that illustrate the major theme. The first section deals with the human body. It looks at the world of sports science, showing what it takes to reach the very pinnacle of human performance. It also introduces people with abilities that might even be classed as 'superhuman'. In the second section, we examine developments in health and medicine. We investigate how scientists are attempting to combat serious health problems like antibiotic resistance and mosquito-borne diseases, while also turning to more everyday issues such as boredom, creativity, and sleep. The third section concerns the very important issue of nature and the environment. We dive into the Great Pacific Garbage Patch and examine its implications for our use of plastics and recycling. We learn about efforts to solve food shortages by growing crops in the desert, and get a glimpse of the scientific work being carried out in the frozen wastes of Antarctica. The fourth section is about the universe. Will human beings ever colonize Mars? Is a mysterious star in the universe evidence of alien life? Have humans caused environmental problems in space too? Finally, we reach the fifth and final section, entitled *Future Inspirations*. Here we look at some other cutting-edge advances in science, including quantum computers, high-speed transportation, and high-tech clothing.

To guide students through the topics introduced in the book, each unit has a number of different activities for them to complete. They consist of two vocabulary exercises, one pre-reading and the other post-reading, which give them practice in using the key terms introduced in the article. There are also two reading activities, designed to test the students' comprehension of both details and main ideas. Following this is a grammar activity which helps students to increase the complexity and accuracy of their sentence building, and a listening exercise that helps them learn the art of summarizing. The unit ends with a pair of discussion questions which encourage students to use their own experiences to think beyond the topic. Thank you for taking an interest in this book. I hope you enjoy using it!

Dave Rear

Science Arena

目次
Table of Contents

Section I: **Human Beings**

Section II: **Health**

Section III : **Nature**

Section IV : **Space**

Section V : **Future Inspirations**

Section I

....

Human Beings

UNIT 1

Real-Life Superhumans

あなたの周りにいる超能力者たち

スパイダーマンや X-MEN のような超能力を持つ人間は、SF 映画の中だけの存在なのでしょうか。実は私たちの住むこの世界にも、そのような能力を持つ人々が存在するのです。それらの人々には、どのような超能力が備わっているのか、また、どのようにその能力を得たのかをご紹介しましょう。

Key Vocabulary

次の単語について、その定義を結びつけましょう。

1. discover   (a) a problem or fault that makes something not perfect

2. ability   (b) to find or invent something new

3. regard   (c) to change to fit a new situation

4. defect   (d) a power or skill to do something

5. adapt   (e) to view something in a particular way

Reading

 1-2〜6

CD1-2 Have you ever dreamed of having a superpower? Do you wish you could fly like Superman, climb like Spider-Man, or run like the Flash? Or perhaps you'd like to be able to transport yourself instantly from one place to another so you would never be late for class? Unfortunately, superheroes only exist in science fiction. Or do they?

5 As a matter of fact, around the world scientists have discovered a surprising number

of people who possess abilities that might be regarded as superhuman.

`CD1-3` Take Liam Hoekstra in the United States, for example. When Liam was just five months old, he was not only able to walk, he could support his entire body on his arms. Less than a year later, he was pushing heavy furniture around his house, lifting weights, and climbing ropes in his local gym. He could eat constantly without 10 gaining weight and had almost no body fat. It turned out that Liam's super strength had come about through a genetic mutation, rather like the X-Men we see in the movies. He was diagnosed with a rare condition which leads to a lack of proteins that regulate muscle development. Now Liam is 15 years-old and, since there are fortunately no health problems associated with his condition, he is free to enjoy a 15 normal life with his family and friends.

`CD1-4` Genetic mutation has given rise to other superhuman abilities too. In Pakistan, researchers discovered a street performer who could cut himself with knives without feeling pain. His condition was caused by a defect in the SCN9A gene, which meant pain did not flow from the nerves to the brain. Scientists hope that the 20 discovery might help them to find a way to treat people suffering from chronic pain.

`CD1-5` Another group of superhumans are the Bajau Laut people from south-east Asia, who spend all their lives in houseboats or villages built on top of coral reefs almost two kilometers out to sea. They spend 60 percent of their time in or under the water, which is the equivalent to a sea otter. Making their living from free-diving 25 fishing, these so-called 'human fish' can descend 20 meters to the ocean floor without scuba equipment and hold their breath for five minutes by slowing their heartbeats to 30 beats per minute. Many of their children have eyes that have adapted to the sea, enabling them to see twice as clearly under water as normal people.

`CD1-6` These are just a few examples of people around the world in possession 30 of what might be considered as superhuman powers. So next time you watch a superhero movie on television, just think. Someday you might get to meet one in real life.

---

note　genetic mutation 遺伝子の突然変異　**diagnose** 診断する　**condition** 病状，病気
　　　　protein タンパク質　**chronic** 慢性の　**sea otter** ラッコ

Reading Comprehension

次の文が本文の内容と一致する場合 T、一致しない場合は F を記入しましょう。

1. (　　) Although some people have special abilities, they shouldn't be regarded as superhuman.
2. (　　) It became clear that Liam Hoekstra had amazing strength even when he was a baby.
3. (　　) Liam gained his strength by training hard in the gym.
4. (　　) The gene SCN9A might be a key for helping people who suffer from untreatable pain.
5. (　　) The Bajau Laut are able to breathe under water thanks to a genetic mutation in their lungs.

Finding Details

次の質問に英語で答えましょう。

1. As well as walking, what could Liam Hoekstra do before he was one year old?

_____

2. What is the function of the SCN9A gene?

_____

3. What are the children of the Bajau Laut able to do better than ordinary people?

_____

Vocabulary in Context

次の英文の空所に入れるのに正しい語句を下から選びましょう。

1. Scientists hope that the discovery could (　　　　　　　) a new way to treat chronic pain.
2. Since it is such a rare (　　　　　　　), doctors do not yet understand it fully.
3. After a lot of research, the cause of the superhuman ability was found to be (　　　　　　　).
4. The new machine should (　　　　　　　) the factory to produce goods much more quickly.
5. 100° Celsius is (　　　　　　　) to 212° Fahrenheit.

genetic	condition	lead to	equivalent to	enable

4

 Writing

次の英文の ▢▢▢▢ 内の単語を並び替えて、意味の通る文にしましょう。

1. 科学者たちは、超人的な能力を持つと思われる人々の発見に驚いた。
Scientists were surprised to find abilities   people   superhuman   seem   who
  possess   to .

_____

_____

2. バジャウ・ラウトの人々は、長い時間息を止めるために心拍数を減らす。
The Bajau Laut people slow their to   heartbeats   hold   in   breath   order
  their for a long time.

_____

_____

3. 遺伝子の突然変異の結果、彼は痛みを感じることなく自分に切り傷をつけることができる。
As a result of a genetic mutation, he experiencing   without   could   himself
  cut   pain .

_____

_____

Listening Summary

🎧 1-7

次の英文を聞いて、空所を埋めましょう。

Superhumans come from science fiction and 1)_____ in the
real world. Or do they? Surprisingly enough, there are a number of people around
the world who 2) _____ that could be classed as superhuman.
One of these people is Liam Hoekstra, a young boy who gained super strength even
when he was just a baby. The reason for Liam's super strength was 3) _____
_____ which meant that he lacked proteins that control muscle development.
Another superhuman also gained his ability from a genetic mutation. This was a
street performer in Pakistan who 4) _____ with knives without
feeling any pain. A third group of people are the Bajau Laut in south-east Asia.
They spend as much time under the water as sea otters, and over time 5) _____
_____ themselves to their lifestyle by learning to dive to the ocean floor and
6) _____ for long periods. You never know, one day you might
meet a real-life superhero.

Express your Ideas

次の英文を読んで、自分の考えを書きましょう。

1. Which of the three examples of superhumans in the article surprised you the most?

_____

_____

_____

2. If you could have any superpower, what superpower would you like to have and why?

_____

_____

_____

The 10,000-hour Rule

1万時間の法則

メッシやロナルドのようなスーパースターの才能は、どこから生まれたので
しょうか。ある心理学者はその秘密を発見しました。サッカー選手からバイ
オリニストまで、天才と呼ばれる人々には、ある共通点が存在したのです。

Key Vocabulary

次の単語について、その定義を結びつけましょう。

1. concept   **(a)** to tell someone a fact they may not have realized

2. confirm   **(b)** to guess a size or value

3. point out   **(c)** an idea or theory

4. misunderstand   **(d)** to get the wrong idea about something

5. estimate   **(e)** to show that something is true

Reading   1-8〜11

CD1-8 Most people will be familiar with the concept of "practice makes perfect". It's
a logical idea: the more you practice something, the better you will get at it. But how
much practice do you need to become a truly expert practitioner? What does it take
to become a world-class footballer, chess player, or classical musician? In 1973, a
pair of American psychology professors, Herbert Simon and William Chase, claimed   5

to have found the answer. Based on a study of chess players, they discovered that not one single grandmaster—the term used in chess for an expert player—had reached that level of performance without doing at least a decade of practice. Chess players are often regarded as geniuses. But geniuses, the study suggested, are not born but
10 *made*.

CD1-9 Since Simon and Chase's famous paper, a number of studies have been carried out that appear to confirm their basic conclusion. When the psychologist John Hayes examined 76 famous classical composers, he found that, in almost every case, their greatest work was not created until they had been composing for at least
15 10 years. In a study by Anders Ericsson of violin players at the elite Music Academy of West Berlin, it was found that the very top violinists, on average and over time, practiced around 30 percent more than the merely "good" ones. On average, the amount of practice they needed to do in order to reach the top was approximately 10,000 hours. In the sports world, a former British table tennis player, Matthew Syed,
20 pointed out that during his career in the 1990s over half of the top-ranked British players, including himself, were all born on the same street. They succeeded because an experienced coach happened to open a club in the neighborhood, allowing them access to high-level practice.

CD1-10 Having said all this, it is important not to misunderstand what the 10,000-
25 hour rule means. It does not mean that with 10,000 hours of practice anyone can become expert at anything. Natural, innate talent is still a large part of the formula. Not everyone is born with the magic feet of Lionel Messi or the hand-eye coordination of Roger Federer. What it does mean, however, is that without a lot of practice, even Messi or Federer would not have become the world-class performers
30 they are. As Malcolm Gladwell wrote in his book *Outliers*, "achievement is talent plus preparation."

CD1-11 The importance of practice also has implications for language learning. No matter how intelligent you are, you cannot become proficient in a foreign language without hard work. The U.S. State Department estimates that for a native English
35 speaker, it takes at least 2,200 hours of study to become fluent in a language like Japanese or Chinese. Unfortunately for busy students, there is no shortcut to becoming an expert.

---

note   practitioner 実践者、練習生   psychology 心理学   innate 生まれながらの
hand-eye coordination 反射神経   implications 影響   proficient 熟達した、堪能な

Reading Comprehension

次の文が本文の内容と一致する場合 T、一致しない場合は F を記入しましょう。

1. (　　) The study by Herbert Simon and William Chase suggested that genius is based on hard work.
2. (　　) A study of violin players found that the "good" violinists practiced for about 10,000 hours.
3. (　　) In the 1990s, 50 percent of top British table tennis players had all grown up in the same neighborhood.
4. (　　) Natural talent is not an important factor in a person's sporting success.
5. (　　) In language learning, it is impossible to become fluent without doing plenty of study.

Finding Details

次の質問に英語で答えましょう。

1. What do chess grandmasters and classical composers have in common, according to the article?

_____

2. According to the study by Anders Ericsson, what caused the gap between the top violinists and the "good" ones?

_____

3. What did Malcolm Gladwell say are the two necessary ingredients for achieving top-level success?

_____

Vocabulary in Context

次の英文の空所に入れるのに正しい語句を下から選びましょう。

1. The chess player practiced for (　　　　　) 10 years to reach this level of ability.
2. What does this research (　　　　　) for people learning a foreign language?
3. The psychologists (　　　　　) the background of expert practitioners in chess, music, and sports.
4. The study had (　　　　　) for a wide range of academic fields.
5. He loves travelling and is (　　　　　) in more than 10 languages.

fluent	examined	approximately	mean	implications

Writing

次の英文の ▓▓▓▓▓ 内の単語を並び替えて、意味の通る文にしましょう。

1. 彼らは経験豊富なコーチと懸命にトレーニングし、ハイレベルな能力に達することができた。

They trained hard with an experienced coach, reach of allowing to high them a level ability.

_____

_____

2. グランドマスターは天才と見なされていたが、彼はその秘密は彼が行った練習の量にあると主張した。

The grandmaster was regarded as a genius, but he claimed his secret practice did was amount the of he .

_____

_____

3. どんなに才能があっても、多大な努力なしでは成功することはできない。

No talent have matter how you much , you cannot succeed without hard work.

_____

_____

Listening Summary

🎧 1-12

次の英文を聞いて、空所を埋めましょう。

The 10,000-hour rule has become a ¹⁾ _____ in the field of sports, music and other skilled activities. ²⁾ _____ originally on the work of two psychologists named Herbert Simon and William Chase, who made a study of chess grandmasters. Simon and Chase ³⁾_____ no grandmasters had reached that position without completing at least a decade of practice. Other studies have revealed that the level of expert violin players is also ⁴⁾ _____ by the amount of practice they did, while a British table tennis player pointed out the overwhelming influence of ⁵⁾ _____ on the sport's top practitioners during the 1990s. The 10,000-hour rule should not be exaggerated, as natural, innate talent is still a very important factor in success. However, the old saying that ⁶⁾ _____ does seem to have some basis in science.

Express your Ideas

次の英文を読んで、自分の考えを書きましょう。

1. What skill (sport, musical instrument, language etc.) have you spent the most time practicing in your life? Have you done any activity for close to 10,000 hours?

   _____

   _____

   _____

2. Which famous sportspeople or musicians do you most admire and why?

   _____

   _____

   _____

UNIT 3

Why are Human Brains So Big?

人間の脳はなぜ大きいのか

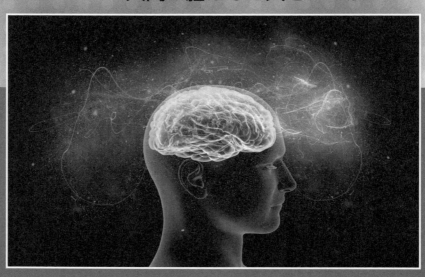

あなたは自分の脳の大きさについて考えたことがありますか？ 人間の脳は、200万年前に比べて2倍の大きさになったと言われています。一体どのような進化を経て、人間の脳は大きくなったのでしょうか。

Key Vocabulary

次の単語について、その定義を結びつけましょう。

1. proportion   (a) a suggested explanation that has not yet been proved

2. hypothesis   (b) part of an animal or plant preserved from long ago

3. evolution   (c) the gradual development of living things over time

4. competition   (d) a part of a total number or amount

5. fossil   (e) a situation in which someone is trying to win against others

Reading

 1-13〜18

CD1-13 Have you ever wondered why you're so smart? As a proportion of body weight, human brains are larger than those of any other creature on Earth. Moreover, since the emergence of the first species of human, *Homo habilis*, about two million years ago, our brains appear to have doubled in size. What accounts for this dramatic
5 increase?

CD1-14 There are no certain answers to this question. One hypothesis is that brain power was boosted by the need for early humans to adapt to changing landscapes and weather conditions. Environmental changes occurred both as a result of large-scale shifts in the global climate and from the migration of humans away from their original homes in equatorial Africa into colder regions north and south. The evolution of a larger brain allowed humans to adapt more successfully to these changing conditions. 10

CD1-15 A second explanation is that, as humans began to increase in number, there was more competition for resources such as food and water in the areas in which they settled. Humans with comparatively greater brain power had an upper hand in the fight for resources, allowing their offspring to survive in larger numbers. Those with less brain power gradually died off, resulting in an evolutionary trend of human brains growing in size over time. 15

CD1-16 While proving one theory over another is very difficult, the so-called "social competition" hypothesis does have a growing body of scientific evidence to support it. Professor David Geary from the University of Missouri analyzed 175 skull fossils dating back from 10,000 to two million years ago. He correlated the size of each skull with multiple other factors, including the likely temperature, environment, and population density of the region in which it was discovered. He found that by far the strongest correlation was with population density. "In fact," Geary said, "it seemed that there was very little change in brain size across our sample of fossil skulls until we hit a certain population size. Once that population density was hit, there was a very quick increase in brain size." 20 25

CD1-17 There is still a great deal we do not know about how human beings evolved. Along with the environmental and social factors described above, scientists also believe diet could have played a role in creating our impressive brain power. The brain consumes 20 percent of the energy produced in the human body, far more than any other organ. The discovery of fire by our ancestors allowed more types of food to be eaten, giving the body more energy that could be provided to its hungriest organ. It also reduced the amount of harmful bacteria we were exposed to, meaning that less of our body's energy was lost to fighting infections and illnesses. 30 35

CD1-18 Our incredible brain power is the one thing that separates us from other animals on this planet. So, next time you score 100 percent on a test, remember this: it all started over two million years ago.

---

note ....

emergence 出現、発生　**migration** 移動、移住　**equatorial** 赤道直下の
offspring 子、子孫　**correlate** 〜の相互関係を示す　**ancestor** 先祖、祖先
expose to 〜にさらす、触れる

Reading Comprehension

次の文が本文の内容と一致する場合 T、一致しない場合は F を記入しましょう。

1. (　　) The human brain has become twice as large compared to two million years ago.
2. (　　) Being forced to adapt to new environmental conditions slowed down the development of our brains.
3. (　　) Competition for food and water increased due to the growing size of our brains.
4. (　　) A high population density seems to lead to larger skull sizes.
5. (　　) The invention of fire might have been another reason why human brains got larger.

Finding Details

次の質問に英語で答えましょう。

1. In what part of the world did the earliest humans live originally?

_____

2. What name is given to the hypothesis discussed in the third and fourth paragraphs?

_____

3. What organ in the human body uses the most energy?

_____

Vocabulary in Context

次の英文の空所に入れるのに正しい語句を下から選びましょう。

1. The higher the population, the more competition there is for (　　　　　　　).
2. This hypothesis fails to (　　　　　　) all the data we have collected on this issue.
3. The gradual increase in brain size was an evolutionary (　　　　　　).
4. Let's see to what degree the two sets of data (　　　　　　) with each other.
5. This is a new kind of (　　　　　　) that we have not seen before.

account for	trend	resources	correlate	bacteria

Writing

次の英文の ▢▢▢▢ 内の単語を並び替えて、意味の通る文にしましょう。

1. 人間の脳は環境の変化に適応した結果として大型化した。

Human brains grew in size adapting a of result to as changes in their environment.

_____

_____

2. 食生活は、人間が脳により多くのエネルギーを供給できるようにすることで、脳のサイズを大きくするのを助けた。

Diet helped to increase brain size humans more allowing energy provide to by to their brains.

_____

_____

3. 大規模な社会集団による、資源をめぐるより大きな競争によって、脳の大きさも増大した。

Brain size also increased greater to competition resources by due for large social groups.

_____

_____

Listening Summary

🎧 1-19

次の英文を聞いて、空所を埋めましょう。

1) _____ body weight, human beings have the largest brains of all the animals on Earth. Why did the size of our brains increase over the past two million years? Although we cannot know for sure, there are three 2) _____ _____. One is that, as a result of environmental changes, human beings were 3) _____ to different living conditions, which gave an 4) _____ advantage to having more brain power. Another factor is the increase of 5) _____ as larger groups of humans fought for the same resources. Scientists have presented evidence for this through a detailed analysis of skull sizes in different regions and time periods. Finally, there is 6) _____ a more energy-rich diet, brought about by the invention of fire. Our brains require a great deal of energy, and fire enabled us to eat more types of food and protected us from harmful bacteria.

Express your Ideas

次の英文を読んで、自分の考えを書きましょう。

1. Social competition might have increased brain size. Do you think it is good to have a lot of competition within society?

   _____

   _____

   _____

2. If human beings continue to evolve, how do you think we may be different in the distant future?

   _____

   _____

   _____

The Advances of Sports Science

スポーツ科学の進歩

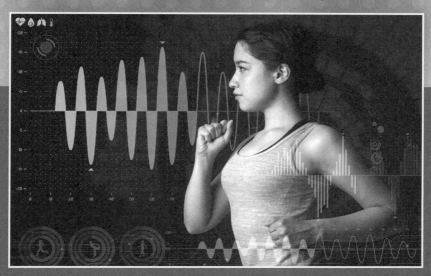

スポーツのパフォーマンスを100%向上させるにはどうすればよいでしょうか。そのような方法はない、というのがその答えです。あなたは100の事柄をそれぞれ1%ずつ改善するのです。それがスポーツ科学の本質といえます。ダイエットやフィットネスプログラムから、フィールドにおける戦術まで、スポーツ科学は現在、世界中のあらゆるプロスポーツの中心となっています。

Key Vocabulary

次の単語について、その定義を結びつけましょう。

1. nutrition   **(a)** the process of getting better

2. precise   **(b)** the food you eat and how it affects your health

3. recovery   **(c)** to help or assist

4. aid   **(d)** to watch something carefully and record the results

5. monitor   **(e)** exact and accurate

Reading

🎧 1-20〜24

CD1-20 When Clive Woodward, the coach of England's World Cup winning rugby team of 2003, was asked how he had managed to turn his players into the best team in the world, he answered: "We just did 100 things one percent better." That, in a nutshell, is what the world of sports science is all about. We have all heard depressing stories of sportspeople resorting to performance-enhancing drugs in order 5 to gain an advantage over their competitors. Sports science, in contrast, aims to help athletes improve their performance without cheating—through harnessing the power of technology.

CD1-21 Sports science works in two areas, which are closely linked: the improvement
10 of fitness and the improvement of performance. In themselves, neither of these aims is new. The ancient Greeks produced essays on health, nutrition, and fitness to help athletes prepare for the Olympic Games. The difference now is that modern technology allows coaches to be much more precise in understanding both what athletes need and how best to provide it. In training, many sportspeople now wear
15 sensors that measure heart rates, blood pressure, hydration levels, and muscle fatigue. They also have GPS trackers that show not only exactly how far they have run, but also their different speeds, changes of direction, and rates of acceleration and deceleration.

CD1-22 All of this data can be used to produce individualized training programs that
20 help to increase fitness and minimize the risk of injury. After a particularly strenuous activity, such as a full game of soccer, treatments are employed to ensure the quickest recovery rates. For instance, Manchester City, a soccer team in England's Premier League, has a cryotherapy chamber, which is cooled by liquid nitrogen to –150°C. Players enter the chamber in their underwear and remain inside for three minutes,
25 the freezing temperature aiding the recovery of tired muscles and injuries.

CD1-23 Aside from fitness, sports science is also used to improve other aspects of performance. GPS trackers can monitor the position of each player on the field, helping coaches to coordinate specific patterns of attack and defense in sports like soccer, rugby, and American football. Other technologies are used to improve
30 players' visual processing by tracking their eye movements and their powers of concentration and spatial awareness through training on computer simulators. As Mike Bartels, the research director of a sports science company, explains, "From heartbeat and brainwaves to foot speed and throwing accuracy, we can now precisely measure just about any physiological or behavioral element of sport."

35 CD1-24 Many universities in Japan have opened sports science departments to train the next generation of elite coaches, nutritionists, and fitness instructors. There is no doubt that sports will continue to be an important area of scientific research from now on.

---

note　in a nutshell 簡単に言えば　resort to ～を用いる、使う　harness 生かす、利用する
hydration 水和　strenuous 激しい　cryotherapy 凍結療法
spatial awareness 空間認識　physiological 生理学的な

Reading Comprehension

次の文が本文の内容と一致する場合 T、一致しない場合は F を記入しましょう。

1. (   ) Like doping, sports science can be considered as a form of cheating.
2. (   ) The aims of sports science are very modern.
3. (   ) Manchester City soccer players use technology to heat up their muscles after a game.
4. (   ) GPS trackers are used both for monitoring individual fitness and for improving team play.
5. (   ) Computer simulators are used to boost players' ability to concentrate.

Finding Details

次の質問に英語で答えましょう。

1. What are the two major aims of sports science?

_____

2. How is the cryotherapy chamber used by Manchester City cooled to such a low temperature?

_____

3. What behavioral elements of sports does Mike Bartels mention?

_____

Vocabulary in Context

次の英文の空所に入れるのに正しい語句を下から選びましょう。

1. Sports scientists (   ) many kinds of methods to improve the performance of players.
2. GPS enables coaches to track their players with great (   ).
3. The player's rate of (   ) was improved through intensive work on his leg muscles.
4. Good (   ) allows players to see what is happening around them.
5. Sensors can (   ) many aspects of health and fitness.

measure	acceleration	employ	spatial awareness	accuracy

● Writing

次の英文の 　　　　 内の単語を並び替えて、意味の通る文にしましょう。

1. そのテニスプレーヤーは目の動きを追跡するセンサーを使用して、彼女の視覚処理を改善した。

The tennis player improved her visual processing sensor of the use a that through tracks eye movements.

_____

_____

2. -150℃に冷却された凍結療法室は、運動後にプレーヤーが回復するスピードを速めることができる。

Cooled to −150°C, cryotherapy chambers can player the at accelerate speed which a recovers after exercise.

_____

_____

3. スポーツ科学がパフォーマンスの基準を向上させる重要な役割を果たし続けることは確実である。

It will is that science sports continue certain to play an important role in raising standards of performance.

_____

_____

● Listening Summary

次の英文を聞いて、空所を埋めましょう。

🎧 1-25

Professional sportsmen and women are always ¹⁾_____ to improve their performance. Some, unfortunately, resort to cheating through drugs. For most competitors, however, sports science offers a much ²⁾_____ to success. Sports science aims to harness the power of technology to improve ³⁾_____ of athletic performance. Most obviously, it allows athletes to improve their individual speed and fitness by ⁴⁾_____ their heart rate, hydration levels, and other aspects of health. It also ⁵⁾_____ from strenuous exercise through the use of high-tech facilities like cryotherapy chambers. Finally, it can help to improve team performance via sensors that ⁶⁾_____ of players across the field. Science is becoming increasingly important in the world of sports, and new advances are sure to be made in the coming years.

Express your Ideas

次の英文を読んで、自分の考えを書きましょう。

1. Do you enjoy playing or watching sports? What sports in the Olympics do you like to watch?

   _____

   _____

   _____

2. Do you think we take sports too seriously? Should we use science to improve performance?

   _____

   _____

   _____

Section I:
Human Beings

memo

Unit 1

....

....

....

....

Unit 2

....

....

....

....

Unit 3

....

....

....

....

Unit 4

....

....

....

....

Section II
Health

The End of Modern Medicine?

抗生物質が効かなくなる日

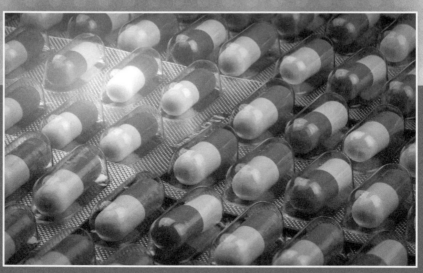

コロナウイルスの発生が示したように、感染症は世界を瞬時に止める力を持っています。しかし、多くの専門家によると、今後はさらに悪化していく可能性があります。なぜなら多くの細菌は、様々な種類の一般的な病気を治療するために私たちが依存している抗生物質に対する耐性を発達させているからです。現在の抗生物質が効かなくなる前に、世界では新しい抗生物質を開発する競争が繰り広げられています。

Key Vocabulary

次の単語について、その定義を結びつけましょう。

1. infection   **(a)** a very small organism that causes disease

2. antibiotic   **(b)** a disease caused by bacteria

3. germ   **(c)** an important discovery that solves a problem

4. breakthrough   **(d)** a quality or characteristic of a chemical

5. property   **(e)** a medicine that cures infections by destroying harmful bacteria

Reading

1-26～29

CD 1-26 If you have ever had an infection in, for example, your chest, stomach, or ear, the chances are that you were prescribed a course of antibiotics to treat it. Until the early 20th century, however, antibiotics did not exist. Illnesses that are easily treated now, such as tuberculosis, pneumonia, and diarrhea, killed millions around the

5 world, and serious cuts could lead to amputation and even death. Alexander

Fleming, a Scottish biologist, was the first person to produce an antibiotic that could be widely used to treat infections. His discovery of penicillin in 1928 dramatically changed the world of medicine, leading to our present era in which antibiotics are prescribed for a huge number of different conditions.

CD 1-27 The problem is, however, that bacteria do not remain the same over time. 10 They evolve quickly and, in some cases, begin to develop resistance to the drugs we use to attack them. In fact, the more we use certain types of antibiotics, the more likely it is that germs will develop resistance to them. There are already a number of infections that cannot be treated with antibiotics, including MRSA, which attacks the skin, and MDR-TB, a form of tuberculosis. In 2015, it was estimated that 33,110 15 people in the European Union died from antibiotic-resistant bacteria, with most infections contracted in hospitals. Such a trend is only likely to get worse. As Dr. Margaret Chan, the former Director-General of the World Health Organization, said in 2017, "The world is heading toward a post-antibiotic era in which common infections will once again kill. This may even bring the end of modern medicine as 20 we know it."

CD 1-28 To prevent this disastrous future, we need to produce new kinds of antibiotics that bacteria do not have resistance to. Unfortunately, this is a very difficult and expensive process. In fact, in the past three decades, no new antibiotics have been created at all. That said, research into antibiotics is continuing, and there is hope that 25 breakthroughs will be made. In 2015, scientists announced the discovery of a new way to produce antibiotics by growing bacteria inside soil. Chemicals produced by the soil bacteria were tested for antibiotic properties, and so far the results have been very promising.

CD 1-29 Even with these soil bacteria, however, it may be some time before new 30 antibiotics are ready to come onto the market. Once they do, the challenge will be to stop doctors from prescribing them too much, since over-use of antibiotics is what leads to the development of resistance. The world of modern medicine is in a difficult place right now, and it will require cooperation across the globe to bring us safely out of the crisis. 35

---

note **prescribe**（薬を）処方する　**tuberculosis** 結核　**pneumonia** 肺炎　**diarrhea** 下痢　**amputation** 切断　**penicillin** ペニシリン（世界初の抗生物質）　**resistance** 抵抗、耐性　**contract** 病気にかかる　**promising** 前途有望な、期待できる

Reading Comprehension

次の文が本文の内容と一致する場合 T、一致しない場合は F を記入しましょう。

1. (   ) Antibiotics were first discovered in the 1800s.
2. (   ) Before antibiotics, you could die if you cut yourself seriously.
3. (   ) Due to their ability to evolve rapidly, bacteria have begun to develop resistance to antibiotics.
4. (   ) The antibiotics we use today were all discovered within the last 30 years.
5. (   ) By growing bacteria inside soil, scientists may have found a new method of producing antibiotics.

Finding Details

次の質問に英語で答えましょう。

1. What was the name of the first antibiotic to be widely used?

   _____

2. Why is MRSA mentioned in the article?

   _____

3. What is it that leads to bacteria gaining resistance to antibiotics?

   _____

Vocabulary in Context

次の英文の空所に入れるのに正しい語句を下から選びましょう。

1. The doctor decided to (   ) the infection with antibiotics.
2. There is no guarantee of success, but so far the results have been (   ).
3. Doctors must be careful not to (   ) antibiotics too much.
4. Many types of bacteria eventually developed (   ) to penicillin.
5. Thanks to the (   ) of my colleagues, I was able to make a breakthrough in my research.

resistance	promising	cooperation	treat	prescribe

Writing

次の英文の 　　　　 内の単語を並び替えて、意味の通る文にしましょう。

1. 現代医学の時代はアレクサンダー・フレミングによるペニシリンの発見の上に成り立っていると言える。

We can say that the modern era of medicine was by upon built discovery the penicillin of Alexander Fleming.

_____

_____

2. 私たちの抗生物質の過剰使用が、それらに対する耐菌性の発達を引き起こしてしまった。

Our over-use of antibiotics led has developing to resistance bacteria to them.

_____

_____

3. 抗生物質が処方されればされるほど、細菌がそれらに対する耐性を発達させる可能性が高い。

The more antibiotics are prescribed, the will is that more it likely bacteria develop resistance to them.

_____

_____

Listening Summary

CD 1-30

次の英文を聞いて、空所を埋めましょう。

Before the 20th century, millions of people died each year from diseases such as tuberculosis, pneumonia, and diarrhoea. In 1928, however, a Scottish biologist named Alexander Fleming [1]_____ that would change medicine forever. Penicillin and other antibiotics revolutionized healthcare, [2]_____ _____ to be cured easily and serious cuts to be treated without risk. Our widespread use of these drugs has, however, come at a cost. Over time, many types of bacteria have evolved to become [3]_____ antibiotics, leading to illnesses that cannot be cured with present medicine. Many doctors fear that we are heading toward a world in which antibiotics will no longer [4]_____. With no new antibiotics having [5]_____ in the last 30 years, we badly need to find a new method of producing these types of drugs. There is some hope, but the world will need to work hard to take us safely [6]_____.

Express your Ideas

次の英文を読んで、自分の考えを書きましょう。

1. Have you ever had an infection? Did you take antibiotics to treat it?

_____

_____

_____

2. What do we have to do in order to overcome the crisis of antibiotic resistance?

_____

_____

_____

UNIT 6

Can You Get Smarter in Your Sleep?

寝れば寝るほど頭が良くなる？

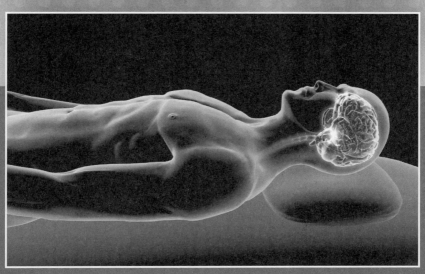

夜ベッドに入って眠ったら、翌朝自分が就寝前よりも賢くなっていたら素晴らしいと思いませんか？残念ながらそんなに単純ではありませんが、睡眠中に記憶を改善するためにできることがいくつかあります。次回、試験勉強するときに試してみませんか？

Key Vocabulary

次の単語について、その定義を結びつけましょう。

1. unconscious   **(a)** a smell

2. transfer   **(b)** someone who participates in an experiment or study

3. odor   **(c)** to move from one place to another

4. subject   **(d)** a particular way of doing something

5. technique   **(e)** in a state of being asleep or similar to it

Reading

 1-31〜35

CD1-31 Have you ever had the feeling that there aren't enough hours in the day? That you have so many assignments to do or tests to study for that you don't even have time to sleep? Well, you're not the only one. That's why for many years scientists have looked into the question of whether it is possible for people to learn while they are asleep. The idea is incredibly appealing. You plug in an audio device, set it to read 5

out a foreign language or the information you need for a test, and then you quietly close your eyes. The next morning, you wake up and find that your unconscious mind has miraculously absorbed the information it was exposed to during the night.

CD1-32 It sounds like science fiction, and, unfortunately, that's just what it is. Despite many experiments conducted over the years, scientists have not found any evidence that the brain can learn new information while asleep. So, does that mean the mind shuts down completely during these unconscious hours? The answer to that, fortunately, is no. During the night, the brain processes the day's experiences and transfers memories from the hippocampus, where memories first form, to other regions of the cortex, where they are held in long-term storage. This process stabilizes our memories and helps us to cement the information or skills we have learned during the day.

CD1-33 This is where science can help us to get smarter. Susanne Diekelmann from the University of Tübingen in Germany has conducted experiments in which participants were exposed to a pleasant odor while playing a memory game. The same odor was then wafted into their room at night, and when they were tested on the memory game the next day, the subjects exposed to the odor scored 84 percent on the test while the control group scored just 61 percent. Diekelmann believes that the odor stimulated the memory stabilization process within the brain and made it more effective.

CD1-34 Other scientists have conducted similar experiments with music and gained the same results. They have also been able to improve memory by stimulating the brain with electrodes. This technique works by analyzing the specific brain waves used during the memory stage of sleep and then giving gentle electric shocks to induce the brain into producing these same patterns. There is even evidence this can be done while the subject is still awake.

CD1-35 Stimulating the brain with electrodes might seem a step too far for busy students hoping to improve their performance in a test. However, the use of odors or music is a technique that anyone can try. Who knows, it could be the difference between getting an A or a B in your next exam.

note ....
expose to 〜に触れる、さらす　**hippocampus** 海馬　**cortex** 大脳皮質　**cement** 〜を固定する、結び付ける　**waft** 〜を漂わせる　**electrode** 電極　**induce** 誘導する、誘発する

Reading Comprehension

次の文が本文の内容と一致する場合 T、一致しない場合は F を記入しましょう。

1. (　　　) It is not possible to learn new information while you are asleep.
2. (　　　) While asleep, information is moved from one part of the brain to other parts.
3. (　　　) If you smell any kind of odor at night, it will improve your memory.
4. (　　　) The memory stabilization process in the brain can be triggered by smells, music, or gentle electric shocks.
5. (　　　) The techniques for improving memory cannot be used by students to improve performance in a test.

Finding Details

次の質問に英語で答えましょう。

1. In what part of the brain do our memories first form?

_____

2. Who carried out the experiment in which participants were exposed to pleasant smells?

_____

3. What is the purpose of giving gentle electric shocks to the brain while the participant is asleep?

_____

Vocabulary in Context

次の英文の空所に入れるのに正しい語句を下から選びましょう。

1. Electric shocks are used to (　　　　　　　　) the patient's muscles.
2. The (　　　　　　　　) in the experiment gained a lower score in the memory test.
3. All our experiments are (　　　　　　　　) in this laboratory.
4. It is not possible for the brain to (　　　　　　　　) new information while asleep.
5. Thankfully, the patient's condition (　　　　　　　　) after the operation.

absorb	conducted	stabilized	control group	stimulate

Writing

次の英文の ▨▨▨▨▨ 内の単語を並び替えて、意味の通る文にしましょう。

1. その研究は、脳が無意識の間に新しい情報を習得することが可能かどうかを調査する。
The study will investigate is for it possible brain whether the to learn new information while unconscious.

_____

_____

2. 夜間にある香りにさらされた被験者は、翌日のテストで見事な成績を残した。
The during were an exposed who to odor subjects the night performed successfully on the test the next day.

_____

_____

3. テストの前日には、一晩中勉強するより寝る方がよい。
On the night before a test, better is than to rather sleep it to study all night.

_____

_____

Listening Summary

次の英文を聞いて、空所を埋めましょう。

CD 1-36

Wouldn't it be wonderful if we could learn in our sleep? You go to bed, set an audio device to read out the information you want to learn, and, bingo, the next morning you ¹⁾_____ it. Unfortunately for busy students, this isn't how our brains work. This does not mean, however, that our brains do nothing at night. While we are asleep, they ²⁾_____ we have had that day and transfer our memories from short-term to long-term storage. The secret to becoming smarter in our sleep, then, is to ³⁾_____ process so that it happens for a longer period of time. Scientists have uncovered three ⁴⁾_____ _____ this: using smell, using music, and using small ⁵⁾_____ _____. For example, if we listen to gentle music while studying and then listen to the same music while asleep, we can improve how effectively our brain ⁶⁾_____ _____ information. Why don't you try it next time you have a test?

Express your Ideas

次の英文を読んで、自分の考えを書きましょう。

1. How many hours of sleep do you get on average? Do you feel it is enough?

    _____

    _____

    _____

2. Have you ever studied all night for a test? Do you think it helped your performance in the test?

    _____

    _____

    _____

UNIT 7

The Hidden Benefits of Boredom

退屈の隠れたメリット

人間は退屈を避けるためなら何でもする傾向にあるようです。中には、退屈するくらいなら、自分自身を感電させる方を選択する人もいるほど。しかし、退屈は実際には私たちに良いことかもしれません。なぜなら、それは通常ではない方法で自分の脳を使うことを強いられるからです。ですからあなたも携帯電話を手放して心を迷走させてみてはいかがですか？その効果に驚かされるかもしれません。

Key Vocabulary

次の単語について、その定義を結びつけましょう。

1. elect   (a) to think of an idea

2. benefit   (b) something that helps you

3. promote   (c) to choose

4. come up with   (d) someone who works for a company

5. employee   (e) to encourage something to happen or develop

Reading

 1-37〜40

CD1-37 In 2014, scientists at the University of Virginia in the U.S. conducted an interesting study about the effects of boredom. In the experiment, subjects were left alone for 15 minutes inside an empty room. They were told to simply sit and think quietly, but, if they wanted, they could press a button which would give them a

5 painful electric shock. Surprisingly, of the 42 people who took part in the experiment,

34

almost half elected to give themselves a shock, many of them several times. One man pressed the button almost 200 times. Human beings, it appears, would rather experience pain than sit and do nothing.

CD1-38 The results might seem, well, shocking; but most of us tend to choose distraction over boredom. We check our phones, play computer games, read through 10 social media feeds, anything to keep our minds occupied. Recently, however, there have been a number of studies which point to the benefits of doing nothing. These studies suggest that, far from being bad for us, boredom can promote creativity and lead to the generation of new ideas. Psychologists at Pennsylvania State University, for example, asked people to name as many different types of vehicles as they could. 15 While the control group tended to think of obvious choices like car or bus, the subjects who had been given a boring task to do beforehand came up with more imaginative ideas, including camel and bobsleigh. Another study asked people to think of ideas for using a pair of plastic cups. Again, the bored group generated significantly more ideas. 20

CD1-39 Being bored forces our mind to create its own entertainment, which can have positive effects both for our mental health and our imagination. Some of the most famous business leaders in the world, including Bill Gates of Microsoft, famously assign a certain amount of time each day to quiet thinking. This type of deliberate daydreaming taps into the unconscious mind and allows the brain to access forgotten 25 memories and form deeper connections between ideas. Studies using MRI scans have shown that the connections between different parts of our brains increase when we are daydreaming compared to during focused thought. Experts recommend activities such as walking to spark a daydreaming state of mind. They even suggest that companies make daydreaming into a regular part of the workday in order to 30 stimulate employees' creativity.

CD1-40 Modern life, with its almost limitless opportunities for entertainment, seems to actively discourage boredom. But perhaps this is not the right way to live. So, next time you've got nothing to do and instinctively start to reach for your smartphone, why not stop for a moment and let yourself daydream for a while instead? You never 35 know, you might end up as the next Bill Gates.

---

note   distraction 気を散らすもの、気晴らし   bobsleigh ボブスレー   assign ～を割り当てる
tap into ～に入り込む   MRI scan MRI スキャン（磁気共鳴映像法）
spark ～の火付け役となる、～に拍車をかける   instinctively 無意識に、本能的に

Reading Comprehension

次の文が本文の内容と一致する場合 T、一致しない場合は F を記入しましょう。

1. (　　) More than 50 percent of the subjects in the experiment chose to give themselves an electric shock.
2. (　　) In the Pennsylvania State University experiment, participants who were bored seemed to show more creativity.
3. (　　) Plastic cups are a useful way of testing how bored people are.
4. (　　) Business leaders make sure they never have time to daydream.
5. (　　) Using MRI scans, researchers have shown that daydreaming makes different connections in the brain.

Finding Details

次の質問に英語で答えましょう。

1. What conclusion did the article draw from the experiment in which subjects gave themselves electric shocks?

_____

2. What task did all the subjects in the Pennsylvania State University experiment have to do?

_____

3. According to the article, what is a good activity to put yourself into a daydreaming frame of mind?

_____

Vocabulary in Context

次の英文の空所に入れるのに正しい語句を下から選びましょう。

1. The manager (　　　　　　　) tasks to all the employees.
2. This type of (　　　　　　　) can move on both land and water.
3. Police do not know whether the fire was started as a (　　　　　　　) act.
4. When we have nothing to do, it seems to be (　　　　　　　) to start looking at our phones.
5. Rather than looking for (　　　　　　　), perhaps we should welcome being bored occasionally.

distractions	vehicle	deliberate	assigned	instinctive

Writing

次の英文の　　　内の単語を並び替えて、意味の通る文にしましょう。

1. 退屈は、決して私たちの健康に悪影響を及ぼすのではなく、実際には私たちにとって良いことである。

Far having effect from on negative a our mental health, boredom can actually be good for us.

_____

_____

2. 空想は、長い間忘れられていた思い出を、私たちに思い起こさせることができる。

Daydreaming memories up our to minds bring allows that have been long forgotten.

_____

_____

3. 退屈を避けるべきものと考える傾向があるが、必ずしもそうではない。

Although we boredom tend think something of to as that should be avoided, this is not necessarily the case.

_____

_____

Listening Summary

次の英文を聞いて、空所を埋めましょう。

CD 1-41

Would we rather experience pain than spend 15 minutes doing nothing? A study by the University of Virginia suggested so when it found that almost ¹⁾_____ _____ in an experiment elected to give themselves electric shocks while sat alone in an empty room. In modern life, we have ²⁾_____ it is easy to avoid being bored. But this is not necessarily a good thing. Studies have shown that boredom can improve our ³⁾_____ creativity. For instance, subjects in an experiment who were given a boring task to do beforehand were able to come up with more interesting ideas than those in a ⁴⁾_____ _____. In fact, studies using MRI scans have revealed that different parts of the brain become connected when we ⁵⁾_____ to daydream. For this reason, experts recommend that busy employees be given time to daydream during their work hours. Perhaps we need to rethink our busy lifestyles and give ourselves more ⁶⁾_____.

次の英文を読んで、自分の考えを書きましょう。

1. Are you the type of person who gets bored easily?

   _____

   _____

   _____

2. Do you think companies should give their employees time to daydream at work?

   _____

   _____

   _____

UNIT 8

Fighting the Menace of Mosquitoes

蚊の脅威との戦い

日本では夏に飛ぶ蚊は迷惑程度の存在かもしれません。しかし、世界の多くの地域では、それらは致命的であり、マラリアや他の生命を脅かす病気を引き起こしているのです。現在、科学者たちはそれらの脅威を減らす方法を模索しています。蚊の根絶は単純な倫理的問題ではありません。しかし、世界中の多くの人々にとって、それは生死を分ける問題なのです。

Key Vocabulary

次の単語について、その定義を結びつけましょう。

1. predator   **(a)** the death of a person caused by violence or an accident

2. fatality   **(b)** a change in the genes of an organism

3. transmit   **(c)** an animal that kills and eats other animals

4. reproduce   **(d)** to have babies or offspring

5. mutation   **(e)** to pass something from one person or place to another

Reading

 1-42〜45

CD1-42 If you were asked to make a list of the most dangerous animals on the planet, you would probably name aggressive predators like snakes, sharks, and crocodiles. But in terms of human fatalities, these fearsome creatures are nothing compared to the humble mosquito. Mosquitoes are responsible for the deaths of around one million human beings per year. By contrast, the second most dangerous animal on   5

the list, snakes, kill barely a tenth of that number, while fatalities from shark attacks usually amount to less than ten a year. The reason for the high number of deaths from mosquitoes is, of course, their capacity to carry dangerous diseases like malaria, dengue fever, and Zika fever, which they transmit to human beings through bites.

10 Over 700 million people are infected by mosquito-borne diseases each year.

CD1-43 Mosquito-borne infections are a huge problem in tropical regions of the planet, particularly Africa. But, through international travel, migration, and climate change, they have also begun to spread to more temperate parts of the globe, including Europe and the United States. In response to this increasing threat,

15 scientists have begun to look at ways they can solve or limit the problem through the use of technology. Their primary strategy involves the use of genetic modification to suppress the ability of mosquitoes to reproduce. Male mosquitoes, which have been genetically modified to make them sterile, are released into the wild, where they mate with females. The eggs produced by the females do not hatch, meaning that the

20 next generation of mosquitoes is significantly reduced in number. If enough sterilized males are released, eventually the mosquitoes could die out completely. Another method involves producing mosquitoes which can only have male rather than female young. This too should have the effect of reducing the overall mosquito population.

CD1-44 So far, tests using genetically modified mosquitoes have been carried out in

25 places such as Brazil, Malaysia, Florida, and Burkina Faso. In the city of Jacobina in Brazil, for example, 450,000 male mosquitoes were released every week for 27 weeks in order to combat the threat of Zika, dengue, and yellow fever. The test appeared to work well, reducing the local mosquito population by as much as 90 percent.

30 **CD1-45** Should we carry out such mosquito eradication programs on a large scale? Some people fear there may be risks to releasing genetically modified mosquitoes that we do not know about, including mutations that lead to new, stronger breeds of the insect. Others point to the impact on creatures that rely on mosquitoes as a food source. As with many kinds of technology, we have to move forward carefully. But

35 for the millions of people around the world at risk of mosquito-borne diseases, genetic modification could be the difference between life and death.

note ···
humble 取るに足らない **mosquito-borne** 蚊の媒介する、蚊媒介性の **temperate** 温暖な
suppress 抑える **sterile** 不妊の、子を生まない **mate** 交尾する **hatch** かえる、孵化する
eradication 根絶、撲滅 **breed** 品種

Reading Comprehension

次の文が本文の内容と一致する場合 T、一致しない場合は F を記入しましょう。

1. (　　) Mosquitoes kill ten times as many people as the next most dangerous creature on Earth.
2. (　　) Disease-carrying mosquitoes are only a problem in Africa.
3. (　　) Scientists are looking for ways to stop mosquitoes from reproducing in such large numbers.
4. (　　) A total of 450,000 mosquitoes were released in the city of Jacobina in Brazil.
5. (　　) There may be unknown risks to large-scale mosquito eradication programs.

Finding Details

次の質問に英語で答えましょう。

1. How many people are killed by mosquitoes each year?

_____

2. What kind of technology is used to reduce the number of mosquitoes being born?

_____

3. In Jacobina, by how much was the local population of mosquitoes reduced?

_____

Vocabulary in Context

次の英文の空所に入れるのに正しい語句を下から選びましょう。

1. Scientists are studying the likely (　　　　　　　) of the test on local mosquito populations.
2. A lot of genetically modified mosquitoes were (　　　　　　　) into the area.
3. Dr. Phillips is (　　　　　　) for managing the overall operation of the test.
4. Infectious diseases can be spread by the (　　　　　　) of people around the world.
5. We must not underestimate the (　　　　　　) climate change poses to our way of life.

responsible	migration	released	threat	impact

Writing

次の英文の 内の単語を並び替えて、意味の通る文にしましょう。

1. 科学者たちは遺伝子組み換えを利用して、蚊の問題を解決しようとしている。
Scientists are trying to solve the problem of mosquitoes modification of the genetic through use .

_____

_____

2. 蚊は年間 100 万人の人間を殺すが、蛇に咬まれて死ぬ人数ははるかに少ない。
Mosquitoes kill a million people a year, who of the while die number people from snake bites is far less.

_____

_____

3. 不妊の蚊が野生に放出され、その地域の蚊の数が劇的に減少している。
Sterile mosquitoes were released into the wild, the to fall dramatic a in leading local mosquito population.

_____

_____

Listening Summary

次の英文を聞いて、空所を埋めましょう。

1-46

Mosquitoes are the single most dangerous creatures on this planet 1)_____ _____ the number of human fatalities they cause. As many as one million people each year are killed by mosquito-borne diseases such as malaria and dengue fever. As global travel and climate change 2)_____ around the world, scientists have turned to technology as a way to limit the populations of mosquitoes. 3)_____ by releasing into the wild male mosquitoes that have been sterilized through 4)_____. When they mate with female mosquitoes, the eggs they produce do not hatch, thereby reducing the number of new mosquitoes in the 5)_____. Tests have been carried out with encouraging results. Is it a good idea to 6)_____ on a large scale? There may be some risks, but the benefits to human health could be huge.

Express your Ideas

次の英文を読んで、自分の考えを書きましょう。

1. Do you often get bitten by mosquitoes? What measures do you take to avoid being bitten?

   _____

   _____

   _____

2. Do you think we should eradicate all disease-carrying mosquitoes from the world?

   _____

   _____

   _____

Section II:
Health

memo

Unit 5

....

....

....

....

Unit 6

....

....

....

....

Unit 7

....

....

....

....

Unit 8

....

....

....

....

Section III
Nature

Unit 9
Growing Food in the Desert

•

Unit 10
Learning from Nature

•

Unit 11
Living at the Bottom of the World

•

Unit 12
The Great Pacific Garbage Patch

Growing Food in the Desert

砂漠での食物栽培

水のない過酷な砂漠地帯で食物を育てることは可能なのでしょうか。驚くべき事に多くの起業家たちがこの挑戦に挑んでいます。砂漠での農業を可能にするのはどのような技術なのでしょうか。そして、その技術は、近い将来に世界が直面する大きな問題を解決する糸口となるかもしれません。

Key Vocabulary

次の単語について、その定義を結びつけましょう。

1. cultivate   **(a)** a person who starts a new business

2. entrepreneur   **(b)** a situation in which there is not enough of something

3. rely on   **(c)** the act of sending out gas, heat, light, etc. into the air

4. shortage   **(d)** to need something or someone for support

5. emission   **(e)** to grow and care for plants

Reading

 1-47〜50

`CD 1-47` Several things come to mind when we picture the great deserts of the world in Africa, Australia, and the Middle East. The chances are, however, that long rows of moist, green vegetables are not among them. Indeed, growing anything in the fierce dry heat of a desert seems like an impossible dream. In such a hostile environment,
5 everything needed for successfully cultivating crops—fresh water, fertile soil, a

temperate climate—is lacking. You might be surprised to hear, then, that a number of agricultural entrepreneurs in places like Jordan and Australia are attempting to do just that.

CD1-48 The technology is surprisingly straightforward, relying on the one thing deserts have plenty of: sunlight. The vegetables are grown inside greenhouses whose 10 temperatures can be controlled by the energy produced from solar panels. The water comes from the sea, pumped to the farms through underground pipes. Solar energy is used to desalinate the salty sea water, allowing the cold fresh water to be used not only for feeding the plants but also keeping the air inside the greenhouses cool and humid. The latter is achieved by trickling the water over evaporative pads on 15 the walls through which air is driven by wind and fans. It is the same method that desert tribes have used for thousands of years to keep their tents cool. When the temperatures drop during the night, the cold water is replaced by warm water heated by the sun during the day. All of this can be remotely controlled through an iPad, so the grower doesn't even need to be in the same country as the farm. 20

CD1-49 As impressive as all this sounds, you might wonder what the point of it is. After all, desert nations like Jordan, which have difficulty growing their own food, can simply import it from overseas. The answer is that it has the potential to solve two of the world's most pressing problems: food and water shortages. By 2050, it is estimated that to match the predicted increase in world population, food production 25 needs to be increased by 50 percent. There simply isn't enough arable land to do that at current productivity levels. As for water, the situation is even more serious, particularly for dry countries like Jordan and Australia. An agricultural method that does not use up any fresh water is almost miraculous and, since it relies entirely on solar power, it produces no carbon emissions either. 30

CD1-50 Whether growing food in the desert can be done on a large enough scale to solve the world's food and water shortages remains to be seen. However, it is certainly an exciting start.

----

note   **moist** 湿った、湿気のある　**temperate** 温暖な　**desalinate** 脱塩する
trickle ～をしたたらせる　**evaporative** 蒸発の　**potential** 潜在力、可能性
pressing 差し迫った、急を要する　**arable** 耕作に適した　**productivity** 生産性

Reading Comprehension

次の文が本文の内容と一致する場合 T、一致しない場合は F を記入しましょう。

1. (　　) Surprisingly, deserts have most of the features needed to grow food successfully.
2. (　　) The water used in the desert farms is pumped from rivers and lakes far away.
3. (　　) All the techniques used in desert farms rely on ideas developed in modern times.
4. (　　) Desert growers can control the system without being physically present at the farm.
5. (　　) Without innovations like desert farms, the world could face a serious lack of food and water.

Finding Details

次の質問に英語で答えましょう。

1. What three things are considered necessary for successfully growing crops?

   _____

2. Where does the energy used in the desert farms come from?

   _____

3. Which global problem is considered more serious, food shortages or water shortages?

   _____

Vocabulary in Context

次の英文の空所に入れるのに正しい語句を下から選びましょう。

1. The (　　　　　　　　) of the farm was raised by using new technology.
2. The land in a desert is not (　　　　　　　　) so special methods are needed to grow food there.
3. This idea has a lot of (　　　　　　　　) so we should explore it further.
4. Countries that cannot grow enough food themselves need to (　　　　　　　　) it from overseas.
5. In this (　　　　　　　　) environment, it is very difficult to grow crops.

hostile	fertile	potential	import	productivity

 Writing

次の英文の [____] 内の単語を並び替えて、意味の通る文にしましょう。

1. 温室内の気温は、太陽光発電パネルを用いて制御されている。
The temperature inside the greenhouses panels is means controlled by solar of .

_____

_____

2. テクノロジーのおかげで、農家の人は自分の農作物と同じ場所にいる必要はない。
Thanks to technology, farmers do not have to be same in as the their place crops .

_____

_____

3. 暑くて乾燥した不毛の砂漠では、わずかな農作物しか育たない。
Few desert can where grow in crops the it is hot, dry, and infertile.

_____

_____

Listening Summary

🎧 1-51

次の英文を聞いて、空所を埋めましょう。

A desert might be the last place you would expect to find ⁱ⁾_____.
However, believe it or not, there are a number of entrepreneurs who are building
farms in some of the ²⁾_____ environments on Earth. The
technology is not particularly complicated, using the one resource that deserts
have a lot of: sunlight. Solar panels ³⁾_____ to desalinate salty
water from the sea, which is then pumped to the farms through underground
pipes. The crops themselves ⁴⁾_____ inside greenhouses, which
are kept cool and humid inside. Growers do not even need to be in the same
country as the farms, since they ⁵⁾_____ everything through an
iPad. With food and ⁶⁾_____ becoming big problems for the world,
innovative ideas like desert farms could be one way in which we protect our
precious environment.

Express your Ideas

次の英文を読んで、自分の考えを書きましょう。

1. Currently Japan imports about 60 percent of the food people eat. Do you think this is a problem?

_____

_____

_____

2. How can we save water in our daily lives?

_____

_____

_____

Learning from Nature

自然界から学ぶ技術

マジックテープ、防弾チョッキ、風力タービン、ソーラーパネル、新幹線：これらの製品の共通点は何でしょうか？答えは、これらすべてが自然界の植物や動物からインスピレーションを受けたものであるということです。それはバイオミミクリーの科学であり、私たちの技術開発のますます重要な部分になりつつあります。

Key Vocabulary

次の単語について、その定義を結びつけましょう。

1. characteristic   **(a)** a piece of equipment used to magnify small objects

2. microscope   **(b)** to be able to

3. manufacture   **(c)** to establish (a new company)

4. found   **(d)** a quality or feature of something

5. manage (to)   **(e)** to produce something, usually in a factory

Reading

 1-52〜56

CD1-52 What do spiders, kingfishers, whales, sharks, and butterflies have in common? As creatures in nature, probably not all that much. However, in the scientific world, they do have one shared feature. They are all animals whose natural characteristics have become an inspiration for new forms of human technology and innovation. The science of copying nature for scientific development is known as *biomimicry*, a word   5

popularized by environmentalist Janine Benyus in a 1997 book of the same name. Benyus showed that by studying characteristics existing in nature, we could create new technologies that add value to our own way of life.

CD1-53 One of the earliest and most famous examples of biomimicry was the
10 invention of Velcro, known as "magic tape" in Japanese. Velcro was invented by a Swiss engineer named George de Mestral after he noticed how burdock burrs became stuck to his dog's fur as they were walking in the Alps. He examined the burrs under a microscope and saw hundreds of tiny hooks that caught on anything with a loop, such as clothing, hair, or fur. De Mestral used this principle to create two
15 strips of nylon, one with hooks and the other with loops, which would stick when put together. It took him eight years to perfect the manufacturing process, but eventually he was able to found a company that sold millions of products around the world.

CD1-54 Along with de Mestral's invention, nature has been the inspiration for a large variety of other products. When Japanese engineers were developing the
20 bullet train, for instance, they found that when it emerged from a tunnel, it would produce a loud sonic boom that would severely disturb nearby residents. With the help of biomimicry, they found a solution to their problem in the elongated beak of a kingfisher bird, which allows it to dive for prey in the water with very little splash. The newly designed nose of the bullet train drastically reduced the noise created by
25 the superfast train.

CD1-55 As for the other creatures mentioned in this article, the strong and lightweight nature of spider webs has been used to create bulletproof vests for the American military, the serrated edges of whale fins have been the inspiration for quiet and efficient wind turbines, and the unique characteristics of shark skin have been copied
30 for swimwear and boats. In the search for more efficient solar panels, meanwhile, scientists turned to the wings of the black rose butterfly, which contain tiny cells that can collect sunlight at any angle. Based on this principle, engineers managed to create a solar cell that is twice as efficient at harvesting light.

CD1-56 Millions of years of evolution have often created solutions to all kinds of
35 problems. Human beings are wise to look to nature for answers.

---

note kingfisher カワセミ **burdock burr** ゴボウの実 **emerge** ～から出てくる、出現する
sonic boom ソニックブーム **elongated** 細長い **serrated** 鋸歯状の、ギザギザの
harvest 収集する、採取する

Reading Comprehension

次の文が本文の内容と一致する場合 T、一致しない場合は F を記入しましょう。

1. (   ) Janine Benyus wrote a book with the word *biomimicry* in the title.
2. (   ) With Velcro, both strips of nylon have hooks on them.
3. (   ) George de Mestral did not manage to sell many Velcro products during his lifetime.
4. (   ) The early design of the bullet train made it very noisy when it entered a tunnel.
5. (   ) The wings of the black rose butterfly can collect sunlight from different angles.

Finding Details

次の質問に英語で答えましょう。

1. What does *biomimicry* mean?

   _____

2. What was George de Mestral doing when he noticed the burdock burrs?

   _____

3. What have spider webs been used for?

   _____

Vocabulary in Context

次の英文の空所に入れるのに正しい語句を下から選びましょう。

1. Scientists based their invention on the same (   ) used in shark skin.
2. Based on the science of (   ), many new products have been designed and improved.
3. The serrated edges of a whale fin help to (   ) water resistance.
4. The natural world has many (   ) that human beings can learn from.
5. The noise of the passing train (   ) her as she was trying to concentrate.

---

features	biomimicry	principle	disturbed	reduce

Writing

次の英文の ███████ 内の単語を並び替えて、意味の通る文にしましょう。

1. 科学者たちは、人間の技術の様々な側面を改善しようと、生物模倣に取り掛かっている。
Scientists have turned to biomimicry aspects an improve various attempt in to of human technology.

_____

_____

2. ジョルジュ・デ・メストラルは、アルプスを歩いていた時に彼の犬の毛に引っ掛かったゴボウの実からアイデアを得た。
George de Mestral was inspired by burdock burrs while to dog's stuck fur his that they walked in the Alps.

_____

_____

3. 重量で見ると、クモの糸は地球上で最も強い素材の一つである。
By weight, spider thread of strongest is on materials the one the planet.

_____

_____

Listening Summary

🎧 1-57

次の英文を聞いて、空所を埋めましょう。

Biomimicry is the science of ¹⁾_____ from nature and using them for human technology and innovation. Perhaps the most famous biomimicry product is Velcro, which was inspired by the ²⁾_____ design of the burdock burr. Swiss engineer George de Mestral created two strips of nylon which would stick when pressed together, eventually ³⁾_____ that sold millions of products around the world. Other examples of biomimicry ⁴⁾_____ by creatures as diverse as sharks, kingfishers, and butterflies. Shark skin has been copied to produce coatings for swimwear and boats. Kingfisher beaks ⁵⁾_____ inspiration for the nose shape of the bullet train, solving a serious problem with noise pollution. Butterfly wings, meanwhile, have been used to create solar cells that are ⁶⁾_____ in capturing sunlight. When it comes to solving problems, it seems that evolution has often already found the answer.

Express your Ideas

次の英文を読んで、自分の考えを書きましょう。

1. Which of the examples of biomimicry in the article interests you the most? Why?

   _____

   _____

   _____

2. What other creatures possess characteristics that humans might be able to copy?

   _____

   _____

   _____

Living at the Bottom of the World

南極で生活するための条件

世界中の人が暮らす場所の中で、南極大陸は最も厳しい場所かもしれません。氷点下の気温、強風、過酷な地形など、世界で最も寒い大陸に関わるすべてが試練に満ちています。では、人々がそこに住みたいと思っているのはなぜでしょうか。

🔊 Key Vocabulary

次の単語について、その定義を結びつけましょう。

1. resident   (a) medical treatment which involves cutting into the body

2. surgery   (b) someone who lives in a particular place

3. shift   (c) activities people do for enjoyment

4. supply   (d) to move or change

5. recreation   (e) providing people with things they need

🔊 Reading

 1-58〜61

CD1-58 Imagine that you had to have your appendix taken out in order to live in your hometown. Believe it or not, that is the price some long-term residents have to pay in order to live and work in the coldest and most remote region on Earth, Antarctica. With the nearest hospital over 1,000 kilometers away, there is no chance to get
5 emergency surgery in the event of a sudden attack of appendicitis, and so the

removal of the organ is the only option for the scientists and military personnel who call Antarctica their home, at least temporarily.

CD1-59 Living in such an inhospitable environment is challenging, to say the least. The temperatures can drop to as low as minus 60 degrees Celsius, with strong winds often making it feel even colder than that. Then there is the unpredictability. Sudden 10 changes in the weather are one problem, and another is the constant shifting of the sea ice, which is always moving, breaking, melting, refreezing, and flowing. Ice shifts can cause long delays to work as supply ships struggle to get through in the changing conditions. Communication and transportation are the third huge challenge in the icy continent. For short distances, the scientists rely on snowmobiles to get them to 15 and from their work areas. But, while from a distance the endless stretches of flat ice might seem smooth, in reality they are covered with tiny ridges of hard snow that bump the machine up and down. Longer journeys are done by helicopter or aircraft, but finding safe landing spots among the high winds and rough terrain is extremely difficult. 20

CD1-60 So, in light of all these difficulties, what is it that makes scientists eager to work in nature's most hostile environment? The answer is that, along with its unique wildlife and star-filled night skies, Antarctica provides a window into the Earth's past. Locked inside the four-kilometer thick ice sheet is a unique record of how our planet's climate has changed over the past one million years, giving scientists a way 25 to measure the impact of human activity on the environment. This has made Antarctica a vital site for the study of climate change, ozone depletion, and sea level rise.

CD1-61 There are usually between 1,000 and 4,000 scientists on the continent at any one time, depending on the season, spread out over 70 bases of varying size. Along 30 with laboratories and research equipment, the larger bases are equipped with sleeping and dining quarters, hydroponic greenhouses, and, for recreation, perhaps a gym, library, and crafts room. Most scientists will remain there only for several months, but some stay for a year or more. For these long–term residents, it is not an easy life, especially in the winter. But, for most, the unique beauty of the continent 35 makes it all worthwhile—as long as they don't mind losing an appendix.

note **appendix** 盲腸 **appendicitis** 虫垂炎 **inhospitable** 荒れ果てた、住みにくい
ridge 突起部 **terrain** 地形、地帯 **in light of** 考慮して、踏まえると
hostile 過酷な、厳しい **ozone depletion** オゾン層破壊
hydroponic greenhouse 水耕栽培

Reading Comprehension

次の文が本文の内容と一致する場合 T、一致しない場合は F を記入しましょう。

1. (　　) Scientists and military workers can get emergency surgery in Antarctica.
2. (　　) The sea ice in Antarctica rarely changes its position.
3. (　　) Traveling by snowmobile is more difficult than it might seem in Antarctica.
4. (　　) Antarctica is a particularly important place for climate scientists.
5. (　　) The majority of scientists remain in Antarctica for less than a year.

Finding Details

次の質問に英語で答えましょう。

1. How far away is the nearest hospital to Antarctica?

_____

2. Why does it often feel even colder than minus 60 degrees Celsius?

_____

3. What three effects of human activity on the environment can be studied in Antarctica?

_____

Vocabulary in Context

次の英文の空所に入れるのに正しい語句を下から選びましょう。

1. Comparatively speaking, the appendix is not such an important (　　　　　　　) in the body.
2. This is the (　　　　　　　) where I conduct most of my research.
3. Antarctica (　　　　　　　) scientists with a unique environment for research.
4. Since the (　　　　　　　) here is so rough, it will be difficult to transport our equipment.
5. Studying the ice in Antarctica can give scientists (　　　　　　　) information about climate change.

| terrain | organ | provides | vital | laboratory |

 Writing

次の英文の ▢▢▢▢ 内の単語を並び替えて、意味の通る文にしましょう。

1. 補給船は、絶え間なく変化する海氷が原因で、南極に到達するのに苦労することがある。
Supply ships can struggle to reach Antarctica constantly   sea   to   shifting   the   ice   due .

_____

_____

2. 南極の独自の環境により、科学者たちは環境に与える人間活動の影響を研究することができる。
Antarctica's unique environment of   to   enables   the   study   effects   scientists human activity on the environment.

_____

_____

3. 科学者たちはそこで働くという挑戦にもかかわらず、大陸を訪れることを切望している。
Scientists are eager to visit the continent there   the   working   challenges   of   despite .

_____

_____

Listening Summary

🎧 1-62

次の英文を聞いて、空所を埋めましょう。

There is one unusual condition for people who want to live in Antarctica in ¹⁾_____
_____ : they have to have their appendix removed before they go. This is because of the difficulty there would be in getting ²⁾_____ in such a remote environment. The southernmost continent is an important site for ³⁾_____ owing to its unique wildlife, clear night skies, and thick ice sheet that has locked in a record of our planet's climate over the past one million years. There are, however, ⁴⁾_____ to living and working there. For one thing, the sea ice is not stable, meaning that it can be difficult for supply ships to ⁵⁾_____ to where the scientists are based. Another problem is transportation. Contrary to our image, the ice in Antarctica is not smooth, so even a short journey by snowmobile can be extremely bumpy and uncomfortable. Life in Antarctica is not easy, but for many scientists its ⁶⁾_____ makes the discomfort worthwhile.

Express your Ideas

次の英文を読んで、自分の考えを書きましょう。

1. Would you like to visit Antarctica? Why / why not?

   _____

   _____

   _____

2. Do you think human beings will solve the problem of global warming?

   _____

   _____

   _____

UNIT 12
The Great Pacific Garbage Patch
太平洋ゴミベルト

1997 年、チャールズ・ムーアという名の海洋学者が衝撃的な発見をしました。160 万キロメートルを超える規模の太平洋ゴミベルトです。海からの漁業の残骸と陸からのプラスチックから成る太平洋ゴミベルトは、大きな環境問題となっています。世界はそれを解決することができるでしょうか。

Key Vocabulary

次の単語について、その定義を結びつけましょう。

1. float   **(a)** the natural flow of water or air in a particular direction

2. current   **(b)** to be made of

3. consist of   **(c)** to use something such as a product or fuel

4. resemble   **(d)** to look like something

5. consume   **(e)** to stay on the surface of a liquid

Reading

 1-63～66

`CD1-63` In 1997, oceanographer and sailor Charles Moore was returning to California through a remote part of the Pacific Ocean when he noticed something he had not expected to see. On every side of his boat was a giant mass of plastic trash floating in the sea. In an article for *Natural History*, Moore wrote, "It seemed unbelievable, but I never found a clear spot. In the week it took to cross (that part of the ocean), no 5 matter what time of day I looked, plastic debris was floating everywhere: bottles, bottle caps, wrappers, fragments."

CD1-64 Moore's shocking discovery became known as the Great Pacific Garbage Patch. The garbage patch, which is the largest of several similar sites in the world's oceans, is caused by Pacific Ocean currents, which draw in trash from coasts and shipping lanes and collect them together into one giant mass. Although it has been difficult to calculate its exact size, it is believed to extend for over 1.6 million square kilometers, making it three times as large as France. It is also growing all the time. The garbage consists mainly of debris from fishing activities, such as discarded nets and ropes, and land-based plastic like bottles, bags, and Styrofoam cups. To make matters worse, much of the plastic cannot easily be seen. It consists of so-called microplastics, smaller than 5mm in length, which are formed when plastic breaks down over time into smaller and smaller pieces without ever disappearing entirely, a process known as photodegradation. Much of the patch resembles a kind of cloudy soup of these microplastics, mixed in with larger items of trash.

CD1-65 The garbage patch, which is believed to exist on the sea bed as well, is extremely harmful to sea life. Seals and other marine mammals can get caught in the nets, while fish can swallow the microplastics, causing these particles to enter the general food chain. The trash also inhibits the growth of plankton and algae, which form the staple food for many species of mammals and fish.

CD1-66 The huge size of the garbage patch and the presence of microplastics mean it is very difficult to clean up. Charles Moore said it would "bankrupt any country" which tried. With no single country responsible for the problem, the cleaning effort has been left to nonprofit organizations like The Ocean Cleanup, which uses a special U-shaped catching device invented by a young entrepreneur named Boyan Slat. Slat's invention does appear to be able to catch even microplastics, but it is still too soon to say whether it will provide an effective solution to the problem. Ultimately, the best solution is also the hardest one: to reduce the amount of plastic we consume in our convenient, everyday lives.

---

note ···

mass 塊　　**debris** 破片、がれき　　**discarded** 廃棄された　　**Styrofoam** 発泡スチロール
photodegradation 光分解　　**inhibit** 妨げる、阻止する　　**algae** 藻類
staple food 主食

Reading Comprehension

次の文が本文の内容と一致する場合 T、一致しない場合は F を記入しましょう。

1. (   ) Charles Moore set out to look for the Great Pacific Garbage Patch.
2. (   ) The trash collects together into a huge mass due to ocean currents.
3. (   ) A lot of the plastic garbage consists of pieces that are smaller than 5mm in length.
4. (   ) Boyan Slat's invention can capture larger pieces of plastic but not smaller ones.
5. (   ) The world's governments are cooperating to clean up the ocean trash.

Finding Details

次の質問に英語で答えましょう。

1. How long did it take Charles Moore to get through the garbage patch?

   _____

2. How large is the Great Pacific Garbage Patch?

   _____

3. Why does much of the patch appear like a cloudy soup?

   _____

Vocabulary in Context

次の英文の空所に入れるのに正しい語句を下から選びましょう。

1. Rice is a (   ) of the Japanese diet.
2. The harm caused to (   ) creatures is very serious.
3. Scientists are trying to (   ) the precise size of the garbage patch.
4. It is only recently that we have been become aware of the problem of (   ).
5. The company went (   ) as a result of the huge costs it had to pay.

| determine | microplastic | marine | staple | bankrupt |

Writing

次の英文の 内の単語を並び替えて、意味の通る文にしましょう。

1. ゴミベルトは、フランスの3倍に当たる面積に及んでいる。
The garbage patch covers an area times as that three as is large France.

_____

_____

2. その装置がベルト内のすべてのプラスチックを取り除けるかは不明だ。
It is not able whether will device be known the to clean all the plastics in the patch.

_____

_____

3. 一週間の間、チャールズ・ムーアはどこを見渡してもごみを見ることができた。
For one week, Charles Moore could see looked no he garbage where matter .

_____

_____

Listening Summary

🎧 1-67

次の英文を聞いて、空所を埋めましょう。

The Great Pacific Garbage Patch 1)_____ by an oceanographer named Charles Moores as he returned to his home in California. The largest of several similar sites around the world, the garbage patch is made up of debris from the fishing industry and plastics from the land that have been gathered together by 2)_____ the Pacific Ocean. Three times the size of France and growing all the time, the garbage patch is extremely difficult to clean up, not least because much of the plastic 3)_____ tiny pieces of plastic, known as microplastics, that have been 4)_____ through exposure to the sun. No government will take responsibility for cleaning the mess, so the work has been left to 5)_____ such as The Ocean Cleanup. The Ocean Cleanup uses a 6)_____ by entrepreneur Boyan Slat. So far it seems to be successful in collecting even microplastics, but it is too early to say whether it will be truly effective.

Express your Ideas

次の英文を読んで、自分の考えを書きましょう。

1. Do you use a lot of plastics in your everyday life?

   _____

   _____

   _____

2. What are some ways we can reduce the amount of plastic we consume?

   _____

   _____

   _____

memo

Unit 9

Unit 10

Unit 11

Unit 12

Section IV

Space

UNIT 13

The Most Mysterious Star in the Universe

宇宙で最も神秘的な星

地球から 1,200 光年以上の距離にあり、2015 年の発見以来、天文学者を困惑させてきた星があります。この不思議な星からの光は、何かが定期的に光を遮っているように暗くなります。何が原因なのでしょうか？そこにはとても刺激的な説明がありました。

Key Vocabulary

次の単語について、その定義を結びつけましょう。

1. observe   **(a)** lasting only for a short time

2. extract   **(b)** not bright or clear

3. orbit   **(c)** to watch something carefully

4. dim   **(d)** to move or revolve around something, like a planet around a star

5. brief   **(e)** to take something out

Reading

 2-1〜5

CD2-1 In 2015, a team of astronomers at Louisiana State University announced the discovery of something interesting. Using the Kepler Space Telescope, they had found a star, more than 1,200 light-years from Earth, which was flickering and dipping in a way that had never been observed before. The dipping, which reduces

5 the star's brightness by up to 22 percent, could only really be explained if something

was intermittently blocking its light. The researchers proposed a number of hypotheses about what this blocking could be caused by, including black holes, groups of comets, and huge clouds of space dust. But there was one more explanation that got people even more excited: aliens.

`CD2-2` Back in 1960, a physicist named Freeman Dyson reminded the academic 10 community of an old science fiction idea about highly advanced alien civilizations. The idea was that, in order to produce enough energy to power their world, aliens might extract energy directly from a star via some kind of massive power plant in space. Dyson suggested that looking for a huge structure like this might be the best way to search for intelligent alien life. 15

`CD2-3` When the discovery of the flickering star was announced, some astronomers realized that the data fit the pattern of a group of giant solar panels orbiting around the star, periodically blocking its light. They also noticed another interesting aspect of the star that fit the alien explanation. As well as dipping intermittently, the star was also getting dimmer over time, losing 3 percent of its light in four years. This kind of 20 dimming could not be explained by, for example, a group of comets passing by. But if there were a multitude of solar panels orbiting the star at different distances and speeds, that could, in theory, dim the star over years or decades, like a slow-moving flock of birds blocking out the sky.

`CD2-4` Naturally, not all scientists support the alien hypothesis. They say that a cloud 25 of space dust is a more likely explanation for both the dipping and the dimming. They also point to another possible answer: that the star is gradually eating a nearby planet in its orbit. If a planet was being slowly burned up, the debris could block the star's light, like the dipping observed by astronomers. When it finally crashed into the star completely, there would be a brief rise in temperature and brightness, followed 30 by a gradual dimming.

`CD2-5` Whether the cause is planet eating, space dust, or aliens, scientists are still excited by this mysterious star so far away from us. Whatever happens, they know they will learn something new from it. And as long as it remains a mystery, we can still choose the explanation we like best. I know what mine is. 35

---

note **flicker** 揺らめく、点滅する　**dip** 浸漬、減光　**intermittently** 途切れ途切れ、断続的に
comet 彗星　**periodically** 定期的に、周期的に　**multitude** 多数の

Reading Comprehension

次の文が本文の内容と一致する場合 T、一致しない場合は F を記入しましょう。

1. (   ) The star is the only one discovered so far that flickers and dips in such a way.
2. (   ) Dyson took his theory from old science fiction stories.
3. (   ) Both the dipping and the dimming of the star could be explained by an alien power plant structure.
4. (   ) The group of comets theory explains the dimming of the star but not the dipping.
5. (   ) If a planet was being eaten by the star, it might create debris that could periodically block the star's light.

Finding Details

次の質問に英語で答えましょう。

1. How many possible explanations for the dipping of the star are mentioned in the first paragraph?

_____

2. What did Freeman Dyson suggest we look for in order to find evidence of advanced alien civilizations?

_____

3. Which hypothesis about the star does the writer of the article seem to find most attractive?

_____

Vocabulary in Context

次の英文の空所に入れるのに正しい語句を下から選びましょう。

1. Technology has advanced a great deal over the last (   ).
2. Could the dipping of the star's light be the result of an alien (   )?
3. There are a (   ) of stars in the night sky.
4. Scientists are trying to work out what might (   ) such a phenomenon.
5. Our (   ) is one of eight in the solar system.

cause	structure	multitude	planet	decade

Writing

次の英文の　　　　　内の単語を並び替えて、意味の通る文にしましょう。

1. 星の減光は、その原因が何だったとしても興味深いことだ。

The dipping of the star is interesting, the turns cause it whatever of out to be.

_____

_____

2. 宇宙人は、異なる速度で星を周回する巨大な太陽電池パネルを作成した可能性がある。

Aliens might have created massive solar panels the different orbit speeds star at that .

_____

_____

3. 時にサイエンス・フィクションは、科学者たちに新しいアイデアへのインスピレーションを与える。

Science fiction can sometimes inspiration for scientists new ideas with provide .

_____

_____

Listening Summary

次の英文を聞いて、空所を埋めましょう。

2-6

In 2015, a mysterious star was discovered around 1,200 light-years from Earth. What makes the star interesting is that its light dips intermittently by as much as 22 percent. Scientists are unsure what ¹⁾_____ the dipping since they have not observed it in any other star. The most exciting theory is that it is due to a massive ²⁾_____ built near the star in order to capture its energy. This idea, which comes originally from science fiction, would explain both the dipping and another ³⁾_____ of the star, the fact that its light seems to have dimmed over the past years. Of course, aliens are not the only ⁴⁾_____. Some scientists believe that a huge cloud of space dust passing between the star and the Earth is a more likely cause of the dipping and dimming. Others ⁵⁾_____ that the star may be eating a nearby planet, debris from which could block the star's light. For the time being, however, the star ⁶⁾_____, and it is one that astronomers are determined to investigate further.

Express your Ideas

次の英文を読んで、自分の考えを書きましょう。

1. What do you think is the most likely explanation for the dipping and dimming of the star?

   _____

   _____

   _____

2. Do you believe there are intelligent aliens in space? Will we ever meet them?

   _____

   _____

   _____

Space Flight for Everyone

人々が宇宙旅行する日

月に旅行したいと思ったことはありますか？十分な資金さえあれば、数年後には、これは実際に可能になるかもしれません。現在、いくつかの企業が宇宙への観光旅行を提供するために競合しています。彼らがそれを達成する可能性がどれくらいあるのでしょうか？また、生産するロケットで他に何ができるようになるのでしょうか？

Key Vocabulary

次の単語について、その定義を結びつけましょう。

1. headline	**(a)** the layer of gases around the Earth
2. deadline	**(b)** the title of a newspaper story
3. atmosphere	**(c)** money received by a company for its products or services
4. alternative	**(d)** one of two or more things that you can choose between
5. revenue	**(e)** the time by which a project must be finished

Reading

CD 2-7〜11

CD2-7 In 2018, Yusaku Maezawa, the billionaire founder of online fashion retailer Zozotown, made headlines when he announced he would be the first private passenger to fly around the moon on SpaceX's planned space vehicle, Starship. In January 2020, he made the news again when he advertised for a female partner to accompany him on the trip, his previous girlfriend having apparently turned him 5 down. He gained plenty of offers from interested women, but how likely is it that Maezawa, and others like him, will be able to make such a trip in the near future? And will space travel ever become a mainstream activity?

CD2-8 Despite the headlines, Maezawa would not be the first tourist to go to space.
10 That honor belongs to American multimillionaire Dennis Tito, who paid $20 million to fly to the International Space Station on a Russian Soyuz rocket in 2001. Six more tourists followed him over the next few years, but since 2009 there have been no others. The huge costs and technical difficulties of developing a safe and reliable means of transport has meant repeated delays and missed deadlines as various
15 companies compete to turn space travel into a successful, long-term business. Now, however, there are signs that this is about to change.

CD2-9 There are three major firms currently competing in the space market: Richard Branson's Virgin Galactic, SpaceX, founded by Tesla Motors' Elon Musk, and Blue Origin, owned by Amazon founder Jeff Bezos. More than 600 people have already
20 signed up to fly on Virgin Galactic's SpaceShipTwo, paying $250,000 for a planned 2.5-hour trip, of which six minutes would be spent in weightless conditions above the Earth's atmosphere. SpaceX's expedition around the moon, with Maezawa and a few companions, would take a lot longer, probably around six days.

CD2-10 Space tourism for the rich is not, however, the only aim of these three
25 companies. Their more ambitious plan is to create an alternative to long-haul air travel. Currently more than 150 million passengers a year fly routes longer than 10 hours. SpaceX has announced plans to use its Starship rocket to fly as many as 100 people around the world in minutes. The journey from New York to Shanghai, for example, takes 15 hours by airplane. Starship could make the trip in 39 minutes. A
30 recent report by the investment bank UBS estimated that if five percent of long-haul flights could be done by space at $2,500 per trip, that could bring the firm a revenue of over $20 billion a year.

CD2-11 Replacing airplanes with spaceships sounds like science fiction. But, with tourist space flights soon to become a reality, a future of space travel for all may not
35 be so far away.

---

note　　**turn down** 断る、退ける　**mainstream** 主流　**weightless** 無重力の　**long-haul** 長距離の
firm 会社

Reading Comprehension

次の文が本文の内容と一致する場合 T、一致しない場合は F を記入しましょう。

1. (   ) Yusaku Maezawa aims to be the first tourist to fly around the moon.
2. (   ) A total of six people have so far gone to space as tourists.
3. (   ) The main reason large-scale space tourism has not happened sooner is that people are not interested in going to space.
4. (   ) In Virgin Galactic's planned trip, passengers would spend a total of 2.5 hours in space.
5. (   ) Space companies aim to shorten trips that people normally take by airplane.

Finding Details

次の質問に英語で答えましょう。

1. Which company is making the spacecraft that Yusaku Maezawa is planning to fly around the moon on?

   _____

2. Who was the first tourist to go to space?

   _____

3. How long is Maezawa's trip into space expected to last for?

   _____

Vocabulary in Context

次の英文の空所に入れるのに正しい語句を下から選びましょう。

1. The (   ) was founded in Japan but now has offices all over the world.
2. The (   ) was delayed due to bad weather conditions.
3. Amazon and Rakuten are two competing online (   ) operating in Japan.
4. Above all else, space companies have to make sure their rockets are safe and (   ).
5. SpaceX's (   ) plan is to use rockets in place of airplanes.

retailers	reliable	expedition	ambitious	firm

Writing

次の英文の [ ] 内の単語を並び替えて、意味の通る文にしましょう。

1. その起業家は宇宙旅行の乗客になると発表した。
The entrepreneur announced [on passenger a he be that would] a trip into space.

____

____

2. 月を周回する旅行は、通常の宇宙観光旅行よりもはるかに時間がかかる。
A journey around the moon [longer would much ordinary than take] space tourist trips.

____

____

3. 宇宙観光は、宇宙企業によって発表された計画の一つに過ぎない。
Space tourism is [been of one have plans that the only] announced by space companies.

____

____

Listening Summary

CD 2-12

次の英文を聞いて、空所を埋めましょう。

Yusaku Maezawa, the entrepreneur who founded Zozotown, announced his intention to be the first tourist to travel 1) ______________. The moon trip is being planned by SpaceX, one of three companies that are involved in the race to make a successful business out of 2) ______________. While the first tourist to enter space made the trip as far back as 2001, there have not been many others who have 3) ______________. The cost and difficulties of creating safe and reliable rocket ships has 4) ______________ in making space tourism available to more people. Now, however, there are signs that this could be changing. Already Virgin Galactic has 600 people 5) ______________ $250,000 to go to space. In the future, companies like SpaceX and Virgin aim to use rockets for 6) ______________ travel on Earth. If they succeed, we may be entering a world where space travel is available to all.

Express your Ideas

次の英文を読んで、自分の考えを書きましょう。

1. If you had the money, would you like to travel into space?

_____

_____

_____

2. Do you think we will be using rockets for long-haul air travel within the next 30 years?

_____

_____

_____

UNIT 15

Could Humans Live on Mars?

人間は火星に住めるか

火星という赤い惑星は何世紀にもわたって人間を魅了してきました。私たち
の太陽系のすべての惑星の中で、それは地球に最も似ていて、強力な宇宙船
なら到達するのに十分近い惑星です。人間はいつの日か火星に恒久的な植民
地を確立できるでしょうか？そのためには、どのような課題を克服する必要
があるでしょうか？

Key Vocabulary

次の単語について、その定義を結びつけましょう。

1. permanent **(a)** continuing forever or for a long time

2. possess **(b)** something that can be driven from one place to another

3. vehicle **(c)** to be made of, consist of

4. composed of **(d)** to not be damaged or broken by something

5. withstand **(e)** to have or own something

Reading

 2-13~16

CD2-13 Human beings have always had a special fascination with Mars. That is why when NASA and SpaceX announced they were investigating the possibility of traveling to Mars in order to establish a permanent human colony, there was a huge amount of excitement all around the world. Elon Musk even suggested the first
5 people could be sent there within as little as a decade. But how realistic is the idea

that human beings could one day live on Mars?

CD2-14 Mars is the most Earth–like planet in the solar system, with a hard, rocky surface and a huge supply of frozen water at the poles. Although no signs of life have been detected there yet, it does seem to possess the basic building blocks that make the evolution of microscopic organisms possible. At the very least, it may be that life 10 has existed there in the past, if not now. Nor is the distance between Earth and Mars too great. When the orbits of the two planets are at their closest, the journey could be made in just 260 days.

CD2-15 That said, however, there are significant challenges in creating a permanent colony on Mars. First of all, there is the problem of landing. The atmosphere is much 15 thinner than that of Earth, which means that slowing a heavy spacecraft down has to be done using rockets rather than parachutes. Currently, NASA is only able to land a 1-ton vehicle on Mars's surface, whereas a manned craft would have to be at least ten times heavier than that. Secondly, with an average temperature of minus 60 degrees Celsius and air composed mainly of carbon dioxide, humans could not 20 survive on Mars without a spacesuit. They would have to create an airtight base that is able to withstand the freezing temperatures and violent dust storms that are common on Mars. It would also have to provide enough space for people to live comfortably. The physical and psychological difficulties of living in a cramped space over a long period of time cannot be overestimated. Thirdly, there is the issue of food. 25 Water could be taken from the poles, where the first settlement is likely to be established. But while the soil on Mars does contain some of the minerals that plants need, it lacks the necessary nutrients and contains harmful toxins.

CD2-16 All these problems mean that it may be a long time before we possess the necessary technical expertise to establish a long-term colony on Mars. The 30 determination to try, however, is certainly there. Whether our aim is to use Mars as a base from which to explore other parts of our solar system or as a way to guarantee the survival of the human race after Earth becomes uninhabitable, it seems likely that one day human beings will become a multi-planetary species.

---

note **colony** 植民地 **microscopic** 微細な、極小の **manned** 有人の
airtight 密閉された、完璧な **cramped** 窮屈な **nutrient** 栄養素
uninhabitable 居住不可能な **multi-planetary** 複数の惑星の

Reading Comprehension

次の文が本文の内容と一致する場合 T、一致しない場合は F を記入しましょう。

1. (   ) Elon Musk believes there could be people on Mars in the next 10 years.
2. (   ) Microscopic organisms have been discovered in the frozen water at Mars's poles.
3. (   ) Parachutes would not be as effective in the thin atmosphere of Mars.
4. (   ) It is likely that food could be grown in the open air on Mars.
5. (   ) The article concludes that a permanent human colony on Mars will not be possible.

Finding Details

次の質問に英語で答えましょう。

1. What is the minimum time it would take to reach Mars?

_____

2. How many challenges to establishing a permanent colony in Mars are discussed in the third paragraph?

_____

3. Where on Mars is the first base most likely to be made?

_____

Vocabulary in Context

次の英文の空所に入れるのに正しい語句を下から選びましょう。

1. We do not have the (   ) to complete this project without outside help.
2. Water boils at 100 (   ) and freezes at zero.
3. Human beings have long tried to (   ) the mysteries of Mars.
4. The scientists were amazed to find the (   ) could survive in such an inhospitable place.
5. There was a great deal of (   ) pressure on the team to succeed.

---

investigate   organism   degrees   psychological   expertise

Writing

次の英文の 　　　　 内の単語を並び替えて、意味の通る文にしましょう。

1. NASA は火星に恒久的な植民地を定住させるために、そこに人間を送ることを目標としている。

NASA aims to send humans to Mars permanent on order to a establish colony in the planet.

_____

_____

2. 有人宇宙船は、現在火星に着陸できるどの乗り物よりも 10 倍重い。

A manned spacecraft vehicle be times any heavier than ten would that can currently be landed on Mars.

_____

_____

3. 最初の植民地は、凍結水の供給にアクセスできる極域に定住させる可能性が最も高い。

The first colony would most likely be established at the pole, a of frozen where could water be supply accessed.

_____

_____

Listening Summary

🎧 2-17

次の英文を聞いて、空所を埋めましょう。

When NASA and SpaceX ¹⁾_____ to send human beings to Mars, the news generated a great deal of excitement around the world. But how realistic is ²⁾_____? On the positive side, there are aspects to Mars that make the establishment of a ³⁾_____ a reasonable idea. It has a hard, rocky surface and frozen water, and it is not too far away from Earth to make the journey impossible. Nevertheless, three ⁴⁾_____ remain. First is the difficulty of landing a heavy spacecraft on a planet with very little atmosphere. Then there are the ⁵⁾_____, poisonous air, and violent dust storms which would force people to spend almost all of their time inside an airtight base. The ⁶⁾_____ effects of this would surely be very hard. Finally, there is the problem of food, which could not be grown with the soil on Mars in its natural state.

Express your Ideas

次の英文を読んで、自分の考えを書きましょう。

1. If human beings established a colony on Mars, would you like to go?

   _____

   _____

   _____

2. Do you believe that Earth will one day become uninhabitable?

   _____

   _____

   _____

UNIT 16

Space Junk

宇宙に残されたゴミ

人間は陸地や海を汚し、驚くべきことに宇宙さえも汚染してきました。私たちの惑星の周りには、高速で周回する何百万もの瓦礫があり、それぞれが非常に破壊的な事故を引き起こす可能性があるのです。それを防ぐために私たちが現在行っていることはどんなことでしょうか？

Key Vocabulary

次の単語について、その定義を結びつけましょう。

1. pollute   (a) an accident in which two vehicles hit each other

2. operate   (b) able to do things effectively

3. collision   (c) speed

4. velocity   (d) to work or use

5. capable of (e) to make water, air, soil etc. dirty or harmful

Reading

 2-18〜21

CD2-18 We are used to hearing about the garbage dumped by people in the world's cities, rivers, and oceans. But you might have thought that the one place human beings had not yet had a chance to pollute would be space. Unfortunately, that isn't the case. Since the launch of the world's first satellite by the Soviet Union in 1957, we have sent almost 9,000 satellites into space, of which only 1,900 are still 5

operating. Some of the dead satellites have fallen back to Earth, but several thousand are still in space. They form part of over 6,000 tons of space debris currently orbiting at high speed around our planet.

`CD2-19` Most of the debris is very small. There are more than 20,000 pieces about the size of a baseball, half a million no larger than a marble, and tens of millions in the range of millimeters. Some of the larger pieces consist of empty rocket boosters, dead spacecraft, and even astronaut's gloves, while the smaller objects come mainly from pieces of broken satellite and other spacecraft. In 2007 and 2009, two events added considerably to the amount of garbage above our planet. The first occurred when China deliberately destroyed a weather satellite as part of a test, and the second was the result of a collision between a working American communications satellite and a disused Russian one, an accident which completely destroyed both.

`CD2-20` The problem with the debris is that it is moving at such high speed, around 48,000 km/h in many cases. At such velocities, a collision with even the smallest object can be disastrous. The risk of collision includes the so-called Kessler Effect, in which one piece of debris breaks off and hits another so that it becomes a cascade. Since we have become so reliant on satellites for communication and navigation, even the loss of one satellite can be a serious issue. A Kessler cascade of collisions could be catastrophic. In order to prevent such accidents, NASA and other space organizations around the world constantly monitor the positions of the larger objects as they orbit Earth. In 2017, they also attached a new sensor to the outside of the International Space Station, which is capable of tracking objects as small as 0.5mm in size. Its effectiveness is currently being tested.

`CD2-21` Ideally, however, we need to find a way to clean up the debris completely. This is the next challenge space organizations have set themselves. Ideas include a harpoon and net system to catch the debris and a plastic sail to slow their descent into Earth's atmosphere. As more and more satellites are launched into space, tracking and cleaning the garbage they leave behind is yet another environmental problem the world has to face.

---

note　marble ビー玉、大理石　**rocket booster** 打ち上げロケット　**cascade** 滝状の流れ
reliant on 〜に依存している　**catastrophic** 破壊的な、最悪の　**harpoon** 銛

Reading Comprehension

次の文が本文の内容と一致する場合 T、一致しない場合は F を記入しましょう。

1. (   ) Most of the satellites launched into space since 1957 are still working.
2. (   ) The destruction of three satellites in 2007 and 2009 added a lot of space debris above Earth.
3. (   ) The Kessler Effect describes a situation in which one single collision causes many others.
4. (   ) It is necessary to monitor not only larger pieces of debris but also very small ones.
5. (   ) Cleaning up the debris in space seems to be an impossible task.

Finding Details

次の質問に英語で答えましょう。

1. What is the total weight of the space debris orbiting Earth?

   _____

2. Where do most of the smaller pieces of debris come from?

   _____

3. What is special about the new sensor that was attached to the International Space Station in 2017?

   _____

Vocabulary in Context

次の英文の空所に入れるのに正しい語句を下から選びましょう。

1. The (   ) accident left a huge amount of debris in space.
2. The team were looking forward to the successful (   ) of a new satellite.
3. Scientists are worried about the consequences of the (   ) Kessler Effect.
4. New sensors will (   ) the debris as it orbits Earth.
5. Large pieces of debris are a problem, but scientists are (   ) concerned about smaller pieces that are difficult to monitor.

> launch   mainly   so-called   catastrophic   track

 **Writing**

次の英文の ▢▢▢ 内の単語を並び替えて、意味の通る文にしましょう。

1. 現在 7 千以上の死んだ衛星があり、その多くは地球の周りを回り続けている。
There are currently more than 7,000 dead satellites, continue orbit which many to of Earth .

_____

_____

2. 私たちが直面する別の課題は、地球の大気圏の破片をきれいにする方法を見つけることだ。
Another challenge clean a we is method finding to face up the debris above Earth's atmosphere.

_____

_____

3. 私たちが衛星にどれだけ依存しているかを考えると、可能であれば一つでも損失を避ける必要がある。
Given how dependent we are on satellites, be loss even avoided of one has to the if possible.

_____

_____

Listening Summary

🎧 2-22

次の英文を聞いて、空所を埋めましょう。

It might be hard to imagine, but the space above Earth's atmosphere is becoming crowded with garbage. Since 1957, we [1)] _____ more than 9,000 satellites into space, many of which are no longer operating. These [2)] _____ are part of millions of pieces of debris, most no larger than a few millimeters, that are [3)] _____ around our planet. The debris is dangerous because of the high speed at which it travels. Even the tiniest piece could cause a serious accident if it collided with an important satellite or spacecraft. Scientists are [4)] _____ about the Kessler Effect, in which a single collision causes a cascade of other accidents that could [5)] _____ the world's navigation and communication systems. To prevent such a catastrophic outcome, NASA and other space organizations are trying to [6)] _____ as it orbits around Earth. In the future, they hope also to be able to begin cleaning it up.

Express your Ideas

次の英文を読んで、自分の考えを書きましょう。

1. What kinds of human activity are currently reliant on satellites?

_____

_____

_____

2. Do you think there should be any restrictions on the number of satellites we launch into space?

_____

_____

_____

Section IV: Space

memo

Unit 13

....
....
....
....

Unit 14

....
....
....
....

Unit 15

....
....
....
....

Unit 16

....
....
....
....

Section V

Future Inspirations

Origami for Science

科学に活用される折り紙の技術

折り紙の芸術は何世紀にもわたって日本で実践されてきました。しかし、今では、折り紙からハイテク設計の問題に対する答えを求めるエンジニアが増えています。折り紙には、デザインに関する多くの利点があるのです。この古代の芸術を利用した製品にはどのようなものがあるでしょうか？

Key Vocabulary

次の単語について、その定義を結びつけましょう。

1. relevance   **(a)** a type of mathematics dealing with angles and shapes

2. convert   **(b)** a way in which something can be used

3. geometry   **(c)** being related to a subject

4. device   **(d)** a piece of equipment, often electronic

5. application   **(e)** to change the form or purpose of something

Reading

 2-23～27

CD2-23 The traditional art of paper folding, or origami, seems to have been practiced in Japan as long ago as the 7th century, when it was used to create decorations for religious ceremonies. Considering its ancient origins, you might not think that it would have much relevance in the modern world of science and technology.

5 Surprisingly, however, a growing number of engineers are turning to the art form for

inspiration in the creation of everything from nano-machines and robots to satellites and telescopes.

CD2-24 The major way in which origami can be useful to modern engineering is in the principles it provides for taking a flat sheet of material and converting it into a complex, three-dimensional shape just by folding. This allows a large structure to be 10 reduced to a much smaller size while enabling it to be easily opened out when necessary. It is an advantage that is particularly helpful, for example, when designing foldable solar panels for space satellites. Origami can also provide ideas for creating objects with greater flexibility and mobility. Engineers combine the mechanics of folding with the mathematics of geometry, using computer modelling to work out 15 solutions to all kinds of complex technological problems.

CD2-25 The list of devices created with the help of origami is extensive. Along with solar panels on satellites, for instance, origami is also used in the design of folding mirrors for space telescopes. Two well-known physicists, Robert Lang and Koryo Miura, regularly apply origami principles to their work on space technology. The so- 20 called Miura fold, for instance, allows a complex shape to be opened out simply by holding on to both ends and pulling. It was used on solar panels for Japanese satellites as early as 1995.

CD2-26 Another application for origami is the field of robotics. Rescue robots that are used to find people trapped inside collapsed buildings after earthquakes or tornadoes 25 have to be able to move through tiny spaces and cracks among the rubble. A new robot known as CRAM combines the principles of origami with the biomechanics of a cockroach to bend and twist its body into different shapes, allowing it to squeeze itself into even the tightest space. Another robot has been invented that can assemble itself by unfolding its body, almost like a Transformer from the famous movies. It 30 could be used for space work or for constructing shelters in dangerous environments.

CD2-27 In the medical world, too, origami has been useful. Its principles have been used to design heart stents that can be inflated to open up arteries and nano-machines that rely on the folding of DNA. As Robert Lang said, "If you look up into space, or the operating room, you're likely to see origami." One day, it may save your 35 life.

----

note decoration 飾り付け、装飾　nano-machine ナノマシン　rubble 瓦礫、破片
biomechanics 生物力学　heart stent 心臓ステント　artery 動脈
operating room 手術室

Reading Comprehension

次の文が本文の内容と一致する場合 T、一致しない場合は F を記入しましょう。

1. (   ) Modern engineers use origami for the same purpose it was used for in the 7th century.
2. (   ) Origami shows engineers how to change a 2D shape into a 3D shape.
3. (   ) Origami allows engineers without a knowledge of mathematics to work out complex problems.
4. (   ) The Miura fold was first used for foldable mirrors in space telescopes.
5. (   ) CRAM was inspired both by origami and by the natural world.

Finding Details

次の質問に英語で答えましょう。

1. What was origami originally used for?

   _____

2. Name two kinds of objects used in space that make use of origami principles.

   _____

3. What insect was of use in the design of CRAM?

   _____

Vocabulary in Context

次の英文の空所に入れるのに正しい語句を下から選びましょう。

1. Through the use of origami principles, we hope to provide the robot with greater (   ).
2. Her work on lasers made her one of the most famous (   ) in the world.
3. Robert Lang tries to (   ) ideas from origami to different kinds of technology.
4. If they (   ) their strengths, the two researchers would make a great team.
5. If we were able to (   ) the mirror, we could reduce it to a much smaller size.

---

fold	flexibility	physicists	apply	combined

 **Writing**

次の英文の 　　　　　 内の単語を並び替えて、意味の通る文にしましょう。

1. 折り紙は一枚の平らな紙材を立体形状に変換する原理を提供する。
Origami a converting principles provides sheet for flat of material into a 3D shape.

_____

_____

2. 複雑な問題は、幾何学と折り畳みの力学を組み合わせることにより解決できる。
Complex problems can be with solved geometry combining by the mechanics of folding.

_____

_____

3. CRAM はゴキブリのように体をひねったり曲げたりして、最もきつい場所に押し込むことができる。
Like a cockroach, CRAM can twist and to the its body into in bend squeeze order tightest places.

_____

_____

Listening Summary

次の英文を聞いて、空所を埋めましょう。

🔘 2-28

It might be surprising to know that such an ancient art as origami could ¹⁾ _____ _____ in the modern world of science and technology. But there are an increasing number of engineers who have turned to it ²⁾ _____.
The lesson origami has to teach concerns the principles for taking a flat sheet of material and transforming it into a complex 3D shape, a process that ³⁾ _____ _____ to be reduced in size and then opened out when necessary. Robert Lang and Koryo Miura are two scientists who have applied origami to their work. They have designed ⁴⁾ _____ panels and telescope mirrors, just two of the devices that make use of the ⁵⁾ _____ origami. Other devices include rescue robots with bendable bodies for squeezing into tight spaces and heart stents that open up arteries inside the human body. Whether it be in space or in hospitals, origami has many ⁶⁾ _____.

Express your Ideas

次の英文を読んで、自分の考えを書きましょう。

1. Did you practice origami as a child? What shapes were you able to make?

   _____

   _____

   _____

2. Do you think that art has relevance for science? In what ways?

   _____

   _____

   _____

UNIT 18

The Future of High-Speed Travel

未来の超高速移動

過去数十年の間に多くの技術革新がありましたが、いまだに変わっていないことの一つに私たちの移動する速度が挙げられます。その理由はいくつかあります。しかし、世界中を旅する速度を劇的に向上させる見通しはあるのでしょうか？

Key Vocabulary

次の単語について、その定義を結びつけましょう。

1. restrict
2. supersonic
3. conventional
4. investment
5. friction

(a) faster than the speed of sound

(b) money put into a business in order to make a profit later

(c) traditional, usual

(d) when one surface rubs against another surface

(e) to limit something

Reading

 2-29〜33

CD2-29 If you consider all the incredible technological breakthroughs we have made over the past few decades, there is one slightly surprising fact. We have not managed to significantly increase the speed at which we travel. If anything, we have actually got slower. In the 1960s, for example, the Boeing 707 airliner flew at more than 970 km/h, while today most passenger jets are restricted to around 925 km/h. 5

Furthermore, the only passenger aircraft to fly faster than the speed of sound, Concorde, which reached up to 2,180 km/h, was retired in 2003 after suffering a terrible crash in Paris.

`CD2-30` There are two main reasons why aircraft manufacturers have not made a
10 significant effort to increase the speed of their planes. The first is the cost of operating a supersonic jet, which consumes far more fuel than a conventional plane. A ticket on Concorde, for example, cost 30 times more than the cheapest flight for the same route. Second, there is the problem of noise. The sonic boom caused by breaking the sound barrier is so loud that Concorde was banned from flying over populated areas.
15 It flew only over the Atlantic Ocean between Europe and the United States.

`CD2-31` So, what are the options for high-speed transportation of the future? One airline company is actually trying to produce a next generation supersonic plane, which fixes the weaknesses that doomed the Concorde. Boom Supersonic, which has received significant investment from Japan Airlines and Virgin, is building a 55-seat
20 jet with three engines rather than Concorde's four in order to reduce fuel costs. It will deal with the noise problem by only reaching supersonic speeds over the ocean, but in the future there is hope of avoiding the sonic boom entirely through quiet supersonic technology being researched by NASA. If NASA succeeds in its project, it could pave the way to a future where supersonic travel becomes the norm.

25 `CD2-32` Aside from supersonic aircraft, one more possibility for high-speed travel is the so-called Hyperloop system, currently being worked on by, among other people, Elon Musk. The Hyperloop concept involves traveling through a tube from which the air has been removed in order to reduce air resistance. The transport capsule would run on magnets, like the maglev train planned between Tokyo and Nagoya. This
30 would cut down on friction, permitting much higher speeds than possible with a conventional train.

`CD2-33` Unfortunately, there are technical issues to overcome with the Hyperloop, including the energy costs involved with evacuating the tube and the impact of seismic movements on safety. As things stand, there does not seem to be much
35 prospect of vacuum tubes linking the world's cities to provide fast and affordable travel for all. In terms of high-speed travel at least, the future may have to wait.

---

note　sonic boom ソニックブーム　sound barrier 音速の壁　doom 運命づける、決定的なものとする　overcome 乗り越える　evacuate 空にする、真空状態にする　seismic 地震の as things stand 現状では　vacuum 真空の

Reading Comprehension

次の文が本文の内容と一致する場合 T、一致しない場合は F を記入しましょう。

1. (　　　) Passenger airplane speeds have increased only a little since the 1960s.
2. (　　　) Noise and cost are the two major reasons why faster planes have not been developed.
3. (　　　) The jet being developed by Boom Supersonic should be cheaper to operate than Concorde.
4. (　　　) NASA has managed to create supersonic technology that does not cause a sonic boom.
5. (　　　) The Hyperloop system requires both a vacuum tube and maglev technology.

Finding Details

次の質問に英語で答えましょう。

1. What event prompted the retirement of Concorde?

_____

2. Why was Concorde not allowed to fly over populated areas?

_____

3. Why might the Hyperloop be particularly unsafe in a country like Japan?

_____

Vocabulary in Context

次の英文の空所に入れるのに正しい語句を下から選びましょう。

1. Hyperloop trains would run inside a (　　　　　　　　).
2. New technology is needed to (　　　　　　　　) the problem of noise pollution from the sonic boom.
3. Supersonic planes may be a more realistic (　　　　　　　　) for the future than the Hyperloop.
4. Conventional trains are slowed down by (　　　　　　　　) as their speed increases.
5. There are (　　　　　　　　) challenges in developing high-speed transportation systems.

| significant | option | avoid | air resistance | vacuum |

Writing

次の英文の　　　　内の単語を並び替えて、意味の通る文にしましょう。

1. コンコルドから発生する騒音は非常に大きかったため、人口密集地域の上空を飛行することは許可されなかった。

The noise produced by Concorde was `permitted so to that not it was` `loud` fly over populated areas.

_____

_____

2. ハイパーループには、安全性とコストの面でまだ問題がある。

There are still issues `in and the of Hyperloop terms cost with` safety.

_____

_____

3. ブーム・スーパーソニックは、二つの航空会社から多大な投資を受けてプロジェクトを進めている。

Boom Supersonic is proceeding with its project, `two received investment` `from having significant` airlines.

_____

_____

Listening Summary

次の英文を聞いて、空所を埋めましょう。

2-34

In spite of all the [1]_____ made over the last few decades, the speed of air travel has not increased. There are two reasons for this. First, the cost of operating a high-speed plane is enormously high. A ticket for Concorde, the only [2]_____ used so far, was much more expensive than for a conventional plane. Second, the noise produced by the sonic boom as the plane passes through the [3]_____ is extremely loud. Concorde was banned from flying over populated areas as a result. Some airplane manufacturers are trying to develop new supersonic planes [4]_____ these two issues. However, while it does seem possible to make supersonic jets that [5]_____ than before, the problem of the sonic boom has not yet been solved. Another option for high-speed travel is the Hyperloop system, which combines vacuum tubes and maglev technology. Unfortunately, this too has technical problems that [6]_____.

Express your Ideas

次の英文を読んで、自分の考えを書きましょう。

1. Have you ever been on an airplane? Where did you go?

   _____

   _____

   _____

2. Do you think that high-speed travel will be possible within the next 10 years?

   _____

   _____

   _____

Computer Revolution

コンピューター革命

コンピューターは私たちの日常生活に欠かせないものであり、毎年ますます強力になっていきます。研究者たちは今、現在使用しているものよりも何百万倍も強力な全く新しい種類のコンピューターを開発しています。一体どんなテクノロジーを使用するのでしょうか？

🔵 Key Vocabulary

次の単語について、その定義を結びつけましょう。

1. install   (a) to use something in an effective way

2. demand   (b) to put equipment somewhere and make it ready to use

3. fundamental   (c) at the same time

4. utilize   (d) relating to the main part of something

5. simultaneously   (e) a need for something

🔵 Reading

 2-35〜39

CD2-35 If you have an interest in technology, you will surely have heard of a supercomputer, a machine with a much higher level of processing speed than a conventional PC. At the beginning of 2020, the top three most powerful supercomputers in the world were: Summit, housed in the U.S. Department of
5 Energy's Oak Ridge National Laboratory; Sierra, also in the U.S,; and Sunway

TaihuLight, installed in China's National Supercomputing Center in Wuxi. In 2011, Japan's supercomputer K held the title of the world's fastest computer. It has recently been decommissioned, but a new supercomputer known as Fugaku has just been built in its place. It is 100 times more powerful than K and, at the time of writing, has regained the top spot among the world's fastest machines. 10

`CD2-36` The huge processing power of supercomputers is used in a wide variety of fields, including weather forecasting, climate modeling, earthquake simulation, cryptology, drug testing, cosmology, and nuclear physics. Despite their speed, however, some simulations still take days, weeks, or even months to complete, and there is always a demand for even faster, more powerful machines. That is why 15 researchers at companies like Google and Microsoft are turning to a completely new kind of computing, which, if it can be made to work, promises to make computers millions of times faster than today. It is known as quantum computing.

`CD2-37` Quantum computers carry out calculations in a fundamentally different way to conventional computers. Conventional computers rely on transistors which store 20 information in the form of a binary code. If a transistor is on, it stores a number 1; if it is off, it stores a 0. For each calculation, the computer processes these numbers step by step by following a set of instructions called an algorithm. The more transistors a computer has, the more quickly it can process.

`CD2-38` A quantum computer, on the other hand, would utilize a new kind of 25 transistor known as a quantum transistor, which is smaller in size than an atom. Unlike a conventional transistor, a quantum transistor could store a 1 and a 0 at the same time, and, instead of carrying out calculations step by step, it would be able to perform multiple tasks simultaneously. The reason it could do this is due to the peculiar nature of sub-atomic particles, which behave as both particles and waves at 30 the same time. They are, in effect, two things at once—like a 1 and a 0.

`CD2-39` Quantum computers are extremely complicated, and it may be several decades before a working model can be built. But eventually they could replace today's supercomputers and take us into a whole new world of computing power.

---

note **decommission** 廃止する **cryptology** 暗号学 **cosmology** 宇宙論 **quantum** 量子
binary 二進法の、バイナリ **algorithm** アルゴリズム **peculiar** 特有の、特異な
sub-atomic particle 亜原子粒子、原子以下の粒子

● Reading Comprehension

次の文が本文の内容と一致する場合 T、一致しない場合は F を記入しましょう。

1. (　　) Japan's supercomputer K is likely to become the world's fastest computer once more.
2. (　　) One of the fields which utilizes supercomputers is connected with finding new medicines.
3. (　　) Conventional transistors can store 1 and 0 but not at the same time.
4. (　　) An algorithm for a quantum computer is likely to be fundamentally different to one for a conventional computer.
5. (　　) The fact that quantum transistors are smaller than an atom is an important part of what makes them special.

● Finding Details

次の質問に英語で答えましょう。

1. How many different supercomputers are mentioned in the first paragraph?

   _____

2. Which two technology companies are attempting to develop a quantum computer?

   _____

3. How many numbers can a conventional transistor store at one time?

   _____

● Vocabulary in Context

次の英文の空所に入れるのに正しい語句を下から選びましょう。

1. A researcher in (　　　　　　　) physics deals with matter on an atomic level.
2. The electron is a kind of (　　　　　　) found inside atoms.
3. Supercomputers can (　　　　　　) information far faster than a normal computer.
4. Scientists are developing smaller and smaller (　　　　　　).
5. Climate science is just one of the (　　　　　　) that relies on supercomputers.

| process | fields | quantum | transistors | particle |

⚫ **Writing**

次の英文の ▢▢▢ 内の単語を並び替えて、意味の通る文にしましょう。

1. さらなる高速化を目指して、新しいスーパーコンピューターが開発されている。
New supercomputers are reaching the being aim of with developed even higher speeds.

_____

_____

2. 情報は、従来のコンピューターが段階的に処理するバイナリコードに保存される。
Information is stored in a binary step which processes a conventional computer code by step.

_____

_____

3. アルゴリズムとは、コンピューターが計算とタスクを実行するための一連の命令である。
An algorithm is a set of out by a carries computer calculations which instructions and tasks.

_____

_____

⚫ **Listening Summary**

次の英文を聞いて、空所を埋めましょう。

🎧 2-40

Supercomputers are an important tool for scientists in many different fields, from
1)_____ and climate modeling to cryptology and drug testing.
The fastest supercomputer in the world at the beginning of 2020 was Summit,
which 2)_____ the Oak Ridge National Laboratory in the U.S.
With the completion of Fugaku, however, the title of world's fastest computer now
belongs to Japan. That said, some researchers believe that the future of computing
lies in the world of 3)_____. Quantum computers differ
fundamentally from their conventional counterparts in that the transistors they
use can perform multiple calculations 4)_____, rather than
step by step as now. This is because of the nature of sub-atomic particles, which
have a dual nature as both 5)_____ waves. Creating a practical
quantum computer is extremely complex, but if scientists are able to succeed, it
could mean a revolution in 6)_____.

Express your Ideas

次の英文を読んで、自分の考えを書きましょう。

1. Do you use a computer in your daily life? What do you use it for?

_____

_____

_____

2. Do you think it is important for Japan to have the world's fastest supercomputer?

_____

_____

_____

Clothes to Help You Move

体を動かしてくれる服

今日の日本が直面しているすべての問題の中で、高齢化は最も差し迫った問題の一つです。科学者たちは常に人々が健康な生活をより長く生きられるようにする方法を模索しています。最も革新的なアイデアの一つは、私たちが着る衣服です。企業は、着用する人に特別な力を与えることで老化した筋肉を補う「スーパースーツ」の開発に取り組んでいます。それらはどのように機能するのでしょうか？

Key Vocabulary

次の単語について、その定義を結びつけましょう。

1. figure   **(a)** a number or statistic

2. inevitable   **(b)** a part of something, especially a machine

3. joint   **(c)** cannot be prevented

4. component   **(d)** to show or suggest

5. indicate   **(e)** a bendable part of the body such as the elbow, knee, or ankle

Reading

 2-41〜44

CD2-41 One of the issues facing the world, and advanced nations in particular, is the aging of society. In Japan, for example, people aged 65 or over currently comprise about 28 percent of the population, and this figure is expected to rise to 38 percent by 2050. This rapid aging will put a strain on the country's pension and welfare systems and lead to a severe shortage of doctors, nurses, and care workers. In such a   5

situation, it is vital for the nation's economic and social health to find ways to help elderly people remain more active in their everyday lives.

CD2-42 Fortunately, technologies are being developed that may make this possible. One of the most exciting is a new kind of lightweight and comfortable clothing that
10 actually helps wearers to move their muscles. The gradual weakening of the body's muscles is an inevitable part of the aging process, with the rate of muscle loss increasing from 0.5 percent per year at age 60 to 2 percent at 70 and 4 percent at 80. The new "super suit" clothing, designed by U.S. company Seismic, boosts the body's natural power via electric motors that stretch and contract in the same way as human
15 muscles. These electric muscles are fitted into the clothing around the joints of the body. Sensors in the clothing track the wearer's movements and software tells the muscles when to activate.

CD2-43 The hard components of the suit, such as motors and batteries, are housed in small pods to make them as unobtrusive as possible. Indeed, a large part of the
20 appeal of the clothing is that it is comfortable and pleasant to wear, a product that, as its designers say, should be something people "actually want to wear, not have to wear." Seismic, in fact, calls itself an apparel company rather than a technology company, indicating the importance it places on style and comfort. In 2019, it introduced its first range of clothing, which should be available to purchase in the
25 near future.

CD2-44 The super suit is the ultimate example of wearable technology, which is expected to become a growing part of our everyday lives in the years to come. Already many people take advantage of fitness trackers that measure distance run, steps taken, and calories burned. More advanced trackers can also monitor heart
30 rate and quality of sleep. As the technology improves, more healthcare functions are likely to be added, including the measurement of breathing patterns, blood pressure, and blood sugar. Eventually, sensors may even be able to pick up early signs of cancer and other diseases. All of these technologies should help us to stay fitter and healthier for longer, a development that will be good for us as individuals and for our
35 societies as a whole.

---

note　**welfare** 福祉、生活保護　**contract** 縮小、収縮させる　**pod** 容器
unobtrusive 目立たない、控えめな　**apparel** アパレル、衣服

Reading Comprehension

次の文が本文の内容と一致する場合 T、一致しない場合は F を記入しましょう。

1. (　　　) The aging of society is a problem that mainly affects developing countries.
2. (　　　) The "super suit" designed by Seismic copies the way human muscles move.
3. (　　　) The clothing requires motors, sensors, batteries, and software.
4. (　　　) The "super suit" can be bought in shops around the world now.
5. (　　　) Recently a new kind of wearable technology was developed that can find early signs of cancer.

Finding Details

次の質問に英語で答えましょう。

1. What percentage of the Japanese population is predicted to be over 65 by 2050?

   _____

2. What happens to the body's muscles as people get older?

   _____

3. Where are the batteries and the motors of the "super suit" clothing kept?

   _____

Vocabulary in Context

次の英文の空所に入れるのに正しい語句を下から選びましょう。

1. The best technologies benefit societies as well as (　　　　　　　　).
2. In an aging society, it becomes harder for countries to pay for their (　　　　　　　) systems.
3. The number of (　　　　　　　) offered by wearable technologies is likely to increase in the near future.
4. The electric muscles (　　　　　　　) automatically when a user moves their arms or legs.
5. Many elderly people will surely want to (　　　　　　　) one of the suits once they become available.

welfare	activate	purchase	functions	individuals

 **Writing**

次の英文の 　　　　 内の単語を並び替えて、意味の通る文にしましょう。

1. 日本の人口の約 28% は 65 歳以上であり、この数は 2019 年に 38% に増加すると予想されている。

About 28 percent of Japan's population is over 65, expected increase this to number with to 38 percent in 2050.

_____

_____

2. 健康の様々な側面はウェアラブル技術で監視することができる。

Various aspects health can by of technologies monitored wearable be .

_____

_____

3. 老化は体の筋肉の段階的な衰えを引き起こし、年齢が上がるにつれ、その割合が増加する。

Aging to of gradual body's weakening a leads the muscles, with the rate increasing the older we get.

_____

_____

Listening Summary

2-45

次の英文を聞いて、空所を埋めましょう。

Advanced nations like Japan are facing the serious problem of an ¹⁾_____

_____. To help elderly people live more active lives, a number of technologies are being developed to allow them to move around more easily. One example is the clothing being created by a company called Seismic, which has ²⁾_____

_____ built inside that stretch and contract in the same way that human muscles do. The motors are placed around the joints and they ³⁾_____

automatically through sensors that track when the wearer moves. The clothing is designed to be comfortable to wear, with the hard components placed in small pods that are difficult to see and feel. The suit is one ⁴⁾_____ of wearable technology, a field of technology that includes fitness trackers and health monitors. As the technology improves, ⁵⁾_____ we will be able to monitor more and more aspects of our health, ⁶⁾_____ for us as individuals and for the societies we live in.

Express your Ideas

次の英文を読んで、自分の考えを書きましょう。

1. Do you know anyone who would benefit from a suit that would help them to move?

_____

_____

_____

2. Are you worried about Japan's aging society? Do you think solutions will be found to the problems it causes?

_____

_____

_____

Section V:
Future Inspirations

memo

Unit 17

Unit 18

Unit 19

Unit 20

- ❏ ability（名）
- ❏ absorb（動）
- ❏ acceleration（名）
- ❏ account for（動）
- ❏ accuracy（名）
- ❏ activate（動）
- ❏ adapt（動）
- ❏ aid（名 / 動）
- ❏ air resistance（名）
- ❏ alternative（形）
- ❏ ambitious（形）
- ❏ antibiotic（名）
- ❏ application（名）
- ❏ apply（動）
- ❏ approximately（副）
- ❏ atmosphere（名）
- ❏ avoid（動）
- ❏ bacteria（名）
- ❏ bankrupt（形）
- ❏ benefit（名 / 動）
- ❏ biomimicry（名）
- ❏ breakthrough（名）
- ❏ brief（形）
- ❏ capable of（形）
- ❏ catastrophic（形）
- ❏ cause（名 / 動）
- ❏ characteristic（名）
- ❏ collision（名）
- ❏ combine（動）
- ❏ come up with（動）
- ❏ competition（名）
- ❏ component（名）
- ❏ composed of（動）

- ❏ concept（名）
- ❏ condition（名）
- ❏ conduct（名 / 動）
- ❏ confirm（動）
- ❏ consist of（動）
- ❏ consume（動）
- ❏ control group（名）
- ❏ conventional（形）
- ❏ convert（動）
- ❏ cooperation（名）
- ❏ correlate（動）
- ❏ cultivate（動）
- ❏ current（形）
- ❏ deadline（名）
- ❏ decade（名）
- ❏ defect（名）
- ❏ degree(s)（名）
- ❏ demand（名 / 動）
- ❏ determine（動）
- ❏ device（名）
- ❏ dim（動 / 形）
- ❏ discover（動）
- ❏ disturb（動）
- ❏ elect（動）
- ❏ emission（名）
- ❏ employ（動）
- ❏ employee（名）
- ❏ enable（動）
- ❏ entrepreneur（名）
- ❏ equivalent to（形）
- ❏ estimate（動）
- ❏ evolution（名）
- ❏ examine（動）

- ❏ expedition（名）
- ❏ expertise（名）
- ❏ extract（動）
- ❏ fatality（名）
- ❏ feature（名）
- ❏ fertile（形）
- ❏ field（名）
- ❏ figure（名）
- ❏ firm（名）
- ❏ flexibility（名）
- ❏ float（動）
- ❏ fluent（形）
- ❏ fold（動）
- ❏ fossil（名）
- ❏ found（動）
- ❏ friction（名）
- ❏ function（名 / 動）
- ❏ fundamental（形）
- ❏ genetic（形）
- ❏ geometry（名）
- ❏ germ（名）
- ❏ headline（名）
- ❏ hypothesis（名）
- ❏ impact（名）
- ❏ implication（名）
- ❏ import（名 / 動）
- ❏ indicate（動）
- ❏ individual（名/ 形）
- ❏ inevitable（形）
- ❏ infection（名）
- ❏ install（動）
- ❏ investigate（動）
- ❏ investment（名）

- ❏ hostile (形)
- ❏ joint (名)
- ❏ laboratory (名)
- ❏ launch (動)
- ❏ lead to (動)
- ❏ mainly (副)
- ❏ manage to (動)
- ❏ manufacture (動)
- ❏ marine (形)
- ❏ mean (名)
- ❏ measure (動)
- ❏ microplastics (名)
- ❏ microscope (名)
- ❏ migration (名)
- ❏ misunderstand (動)
- ❏ monitor (動)
- ❏ multitude (名)
- ❏ mutation (名)
- ❏ nutrition (名)
- ❏ observe (動)
- ❏ odor (名)
- ❏ operate (動)
- ❏ option (名)
- ❏ orbit (動)
- ❏ organ (名)
- ❏ organism (名)
- ❏ particle (名)
- ❏ permanent (形)
- ❏ physicist (名)
- ❏ planet (名)
- ❏ point out (動)
- ❏ pollute (動)
- ❏ possess (動)

- ❏ potential (名 / 形)
- ❏ precise (形)
- ❏ predator (名)
- ❏ prescribe (動)
- ❏ principle (名)
- ❏ process (名 / 動)
- ❏ productivity (名)
- ❏ promising (形)
- ❏ promote (動)
- ❏ property (名)
- ❏ proportion (名)
- ❏ provide (動)
- ❏ psychological (形)
- ❏ purchase (動)
- ❏ quantum (名 / 形)
- ❏ recovery (名)
- ❏ recreation (名)
- ❏ reduce (動)
- ❏ regard (動)
- ❏ release (動)
- ❏ relevance (名)
- ❏ reliable (形)
- ❏ rely on (動)
- ❏ reproduce (動)
- ❏ resemble (動)
- ❏ resident (名)
- ❏ resistance (名)
- ❏ resources (名)
- ❏ responsible (形)
- ❏ restrict (動)
- ❏ retailer (名)
- ❏ revenue (名)
- ❏ shift (名 / 動)

- ❏ shortage (名)
- ❏ significant (形)
- ❏ simultaneously (副)
- ❏ so-called (形)
- ❏ spatial awareness (名)
- ❏ stabilize (動)
- ❏ staple (名)
- ❏ stimulate (動)
- ❏ structure (名)
- ❏ subject (名)
- ❏ supersonic (形)
- ❏ supply (動)
- ❏ surgery (名)
- ❏ technique (名)
- ❏ terrain (名)
- ❏ threat (名)
- ❏ track (動)
- ❏ transfer (名 / 動)
- ❏ transistor (名)
- ❏ transmit (動)
- ❏ treat (動)
- ❏ trend (名)
- ❏ unconscious (形)
- ❏ utilize (動)
- ❏ vacuum (名)
- ❏ vehicle (名)
- ❏ velocity (名)
- ❏ vital (形)
- ❏ welfare (名)
- ❏ withstand (動)

TEXT PRODUCTION STAFF

edited by	編集
Taiichi Sano	佐野 泰一
cover design by	表紙デザイン
Nobuyoshi Fujino	藤野 伸芳

CD PRODUCTION STAFF

recorded by	吹き込み者
Jennifer Okano (AmE)	ジェニファー・オカノ（アメリカ英語）
Howard Colefield (AmE)	ハワード・コルフィールド（アメリカ英語）

Science Arena
最新科学の探求

2021年1月20日　初版発行
2023年3月10日　第4刷発行

著　者　Dave Rear
発行者　佐野 英一郎
発行所　株式会社 成美堂
　　　　〒101-0052　東京都千代田区神田小川町3-22
　　　　TEL 03-3291-2261　FAX 03-3293-5490
　　　　https://www.seibido.co.jp

印刷・製本　三美印刷（株）

ISBN 978-4-7919-7228-9　　　　　　　　　　Printed in Japan